Coo'

Table c

MW01595326

Introduction

Lighthouse Charity Team
Mission Statement

The Texas Lighthouse Foundation DBA Lighthouse Charity Team is a community-based organization in the Galveston County area. Lighthouse Charity Team provides mobile food preparation units and volunteer labor at no cost to various organizations to assist in their fundraising efforts. Marketing guidance and organizational skills for a successful fundraiser are also offered for "community enrichment".

Community enrichment is a broad category that allows us to focus our skills, our volunteers and our donations where they are needed throughout the communities we serve. Our loyal volunteers invest themselves in many of these projects, from raising money for non-profits to participating in hands-on programs for low-income families and the elderly. We look for ways we can make a difference in the quality of life for our neighbors.

Lighthouse Charity Team is a first responder in emergency situations for natural or man made caused disasters.

Introducing Larry Del Papa
and his wife Joan

When Dick and Scott asked me to introduce their book, "Cooking for a Cause," I was honored. We've been a sponsor and supporter of Lighthouse Charity Team (LCT) for twenty years. When it comes to making a difference in our neighboring communities and beyond, our investment in LCT has been highly gratifying. The work LCT and their many hard working, dedicated Team Members do throughout the year is both amazing and inspiring. Their motto of *People Helping People* is exactly what they do, and, they do it hundreds of times a year.

Lighthouse Charity Team is extremely unique in their capabilities, versatility and accessibility. Their vast arsenal of customized cooking and serving equipment they've designed and built is part of what makes it possible. But, as is always true with any successful organization, their people make them a rare and respected community resource.

From Dick and Horacene Daugird's original vision to the tireless leadership exemplified by Scott Gordon, to the hundreds of volunteer team members who donate countless hours of their personal time, the people of LCT truly model the mission of *People Helping People*. In return, the communities they serve embrace and support them while greatly relying upon them.

On the pages of this book you'll meet some of these people. Through their stories you'll discover how they became involved with LCT and what keeps them coming back to help year after year. Dick felt some of the readers of the book might have an interest in creating their own food-focused charity or organization. So you'll also learn about how to do it and get some down-to-earth how-tos so you have a roadmap to do it right.

The book is a journey into how one man and his lovely wife who love to cook and serve others took that desire and paid it forward. They've built it into a charitable organization that feeds thousands every month and has helped other charities earn millions of dollars for people in the local community and beyond.

Perhaps what strikes me as most unique about LCT is the pride always on display by their Team Members. These people give up a great deal of their personal time and many weekends for the privilege of working hard to benefit others.

Somehow the LCT has created a unique environment where volunteers consider it a privilege to be a LCT Team Member. As a business owner I understand how difficult it is to create a positive, fun environment with paid employees. Achieving it with volunteers who give selflessly of their time rather than receive, is truly uncommon.

I've observed the Team Members share a sense of receiving something far more valuable than money. I believe they gain immeasurable pride, respect, team spirit, gratitude, and a sense of being part of something far greater than them.

None of this happens by accident. It is the result of positive, kind leadership and a great culture, both words connected closely to the name Lighthouse Charity Team. They're unique, have huge hearts, an inspiring work ethic, and have created a model of giving second to none. LCT is an organization without equal and we're incredibly fortunate to have them here in Galveston County.

So read and enjoy, knowing the stories and information within "Cooking for a Cause" represents the best of the best and always *"People Helping People."*

Respectfully,
Larry Del Papa
Del Papa Distributing

Why was this Book Written?

My name is Lorraine Grubbs. As a former leader at Southwest Airlines, one of the most successful companies in America, I understand what makes people loyal to a corporation or a cause and what doesn't. The principles and practices I experienced at Southwest became the basis of my consulting business and my internationally published book, *Lessons in Loyalty.*

With over 30 years experience working with top executives from companies across various industries I've taught the principles of loyalty in the workplace. My next two books captured the stories of successful corporate C.E.O.'s whose own philosophy of "Putting People First" earned them a spot on the Top Employer and Best Places to Work lists.

When I met the Daugirds, founders of the Lighthouse Charity Team, I discovered my principles of loyalty were alive and well in this volunteer environment of dedicated people. Their unpaid workforce is as enthusiastic and fiercely loyal as any paid corporate employee I've researched. Through their *People Helping People* mission, they embody the spirit of "Putting People First." As a result, they've made a huge difference in the lives of others.

The purpose of this book is twofold. First, we wanted to capture the incredible story of the Lighthouse Charity Team. Second, we decided to create a blueprint any community, with a desire to give back, can follow to build their own impactful organization. What does Lighthouse Charity Team do? They provide home-cooked, hot meal food service for any local charity who's raising funds. This is vital because food is an integral part of the fund-raising process. For a charity to know they have a partner who'll deliver quality food service at cost to help raise funds for their benefit event is monumental.

Charities value the LCT because they've proven they not only provide quality food, but they deliver it with an awareness of pride and commitment. LCT, a seemingly "small" community organization, has made a big difference: millions of dollars raised, millions of meals served and many people helped.

As they've grown their impact is now felt throughout the entire State of Texas, branching out from their humble beginnings in the Quaker family-founded, friendly town of Friendswood Texas.

Introducing Dick and Horacene

Whether manufacturing a product or delivering a service, smart companies realize the ultimate competitive advantage in today's workforce is their people. By treating employees with respect, you in turn create loyal "warrior spirits," as we called them at Southwest Airlines.

When I first became aware of Dick, he was operating an insurance agency. I often drove by his office wondering what was behind the unique lighthouse structure where his business was located. Little did I know one day I would appreciate the answer to that question which led me to co-author Dick's story.

I finally met Dick through a boating friend, Joe Stanfield. I knew I'd met a truly special person. You will read, later in the book, Joe's story of meeting Dick. It's worth telling because it reflects the way Dick, in his unassuming way, never meets a stranger.

To know Dick is to love and follow him.

- Lorraine

Chapter One

Looking Back - From Backyard Barbecues to Cooking for Charity

Dick Recounts the History

Like all Texans, our cooking experience started with a backyard brick pit where we smoked briskets, ribs, turkeys, and sausage for friends who brought their meat over to us and said, "You guys are such great cooks, would you mind cooking this for us?"

In 1983, my wife Horacene and I owned a shrimp boat we kept at our bay house in Galveston, Texas. Back then my Uncle, Chuck Daugird worked for a school district. He called me one morning and said the district just remodeled a school kitchen and asked him to haul off the outdated equipment. "I'm bringing over a 40 gallon steam kettle," he said. "It's a little heavy, so I'll need some help unloading it." He had a good point; it weighted over 200 pounds.

When I asked him what we should do with it, he replied, "Boil shrimp caught from your boat! It didn't take long for neighbors to start coming over to help clean and cook the catch and we all had fun eating fresh seafood. Little did we know my love of cooking and bringing people together would become a huge part of our lives.

As time went on, neighbors in this seaside community began asking to borrow the pot for their own shrimp boils. We obliged by delivering the big pot in the back of my pick-up truck and soon it became the hit of every party.

The Road to Charity

In 1968 I opened a State Farm Agency in Houston, Texas. As time went on I moved my insurance agency to Friendswood. My love of the water led me to design our building to look like a lighthouse. Because it was different, it attracted attention and my business flourished.

7

"People Helping People"

 In 1984 the Jerry Lewis' Muscular Dystrophy Association (MDA) approached me asking permission to use the location for a pledge center over Labor Day. We agreed. Realizing the event would attract people and they'd need to eat, Horacene and I borrowed a barbecue trailer from my friend Max Bowen and called our friends to help. We set up a food serving station to cook and serve some barbecue brisket, chicken and sausage to the pledge center volunteers and the community. It was a big success.

The MDA continued holding its yearly fundraiser at this location for eight years raising tens of thousands of dollars each year while we served crowds that grew into the thousands. The Lighthouse was now established as a landmark for charitable giving in the Friendswood community.

Soon, Little League teams, Boy Scout troops, church organizations, schools and other civic organizations came to us asking us to help them plan and serve their community fundraisers and celebrations. Along with Horacene and I, the small group of friends and neighbors that joined us to help became the original Lighthouse Cooking Team. When we weren't cooking, we were designing and building the pits and grills needed to handle the large numbers of people we served.

Lighthouse Cooking Team est. 1984

Kitten Hajecate, Dick Daugird, Pennzoil Representative, Joe Reeves

We were primarily using the same heavy 200 pound pot we got from my uncle. Loading it into the back of our truck every time we had an event was cumbersome. We needed a trailer to haul it around. Plus, we figured additional equipment on the trailer would help the cooking process.

I owned a twenty-foot gooseneck red trailer I bought from a student for 750 dollars in my garage, and we figured it would fit the bill. We named the red trailer "Grandma" and put a barbecue pit, big pot, sink and a roof on it. "Grandma" helped us raise over 300,000 dollars.

In 1986 we were invited to compete in the International Rib Cook Off in Cleveland Ohio. We thought it would be a great opportunity to compete against forty championship-cooking teams and make a little money for our effort.

We took Grandma and a couple borrowed trailers and served ten thousand pork spareribs the first day at "a buck a bone." It was extremely hard work. On the second day we sold "two bones for two bucks." This went on for five days. We needed to replenish supplies and went into town for provisions dressed in our best Texas gear.

Our dusters (long cowboy coats) and boots drew a curious crowd. "Come buy our ribs!" We encouraged everyone we met. They came and we sold a lot of ribs.

At the end of the week we counted our money and were excited when we deposited 40,000 dollars in the bank. Then we counted our expenses. They totaled 42,500 dollars. Lesson learned. You can't fly in cooks, stay at great hotels, eat your product and expect to make a profit. It was a lesson that stayed with us.

We decided cook-offs, catering and other moneymaking cooking ventures were too much hard work and we needed to stick to our real jobs. After all, we cooked for MDA and several other charities for a few years now and felt we were fulfilling our contribution to the community.

But, our adventures in the cooking world were barely beginning. Our banker Jerry Quarles liked to cook. He talked his bank into financing and sponsoring an additional trailer to accompany "Grandma" in 1987. We were happy to have the funds to build this new trailer, but building didn't go smoothly.

We used the wrong material and made a structural mistake. It was gunmetal gray with sidewalls and small window openings. The outside was made of one-quarter inch steel plate which made the trailer too heavy. The twelve-foot long pipe pit not only heated up the structure too much, it also smoked us out every time we cooked.

By Monday when we returned to our jobs after cooking all weekend our throats were so sore we could barely talk. We eventually sold the trailer and occasionally saw it at various cook-offs. We'd walk by nonchalantly acting like we'd never seen it before. If it made its new owners happy, we were happy to be rid of it. I hope reading this book will help you save money and avoid some of our mistakes.

We started at the bottom, the hard way. We washed trailers and swept floors.

Our next venture was with Larry French and Pat Allen in 1988, owners of Acme Welding in Friendswood. Larry and I bought two, retired 25-year old rotisseries from the Pappas Family. Acme was going to rebuild the pits and put them on a newly redesigned trailer.

We named the red trailer "Big Daddy" because it was the team's nickname for me. That rotisserie cooked over 100,000 pounds of meat annually for ten years.

Big Daddy Max Trailer

After faithfully cooking over one million pounds of meat we finally pulled the pit off the trailer and installed a new one donated by Jeff Bowen in memory of his Dad, Max Bowen. You may recall Max was our first sponsor when he donated the use of his barbecue rig for our event at MDA back in 1984. His generosity continued over the years until he passed away in 2012. That first trailer he gave us is still in service 28 years later.

Max and Susan Bowen

On our 25th wedding anniversary in 1992, Horacene and I were at a steel company ordering metal for our next trailer. It took us longer than we thought to order the metal, so our anniversary lunch turned into an anniversary dinner. On the way to dinner, I received a call from a friend regarding a 500 gallon crawfish cooker. He said, "Come pick it up for a 1,000 dollars or I'll sell it tomorrow for 10,000 dollars." I couldn't resist.

13

**Ross Benson, friend and great Team Sponsor built "Afterburner",
the yellow one on the left and donated it to the Team. We can now cook
over 15,000 pounds. per day.**

Chris Delesandri & Jeff Smith

Needless to say, our anniversary dinner was postponed as we
drove across town to bring it home. We'd never used one so we
were a little nervous. But, we took it to the first crawfish event
and learned it cooked so fast it outpaced the servers and diners.

It drowned out the music being played onstage due to the screaming sound when the burners, six, three by eighteen-inch tubes were fired up. Still in use today, crowds love Afterburner.

The metal ordered on our 25th anniversary was used to build an even bigger trailer since our crowds outgrew the capacity of the trailers we had. Once again, I went back to my friends Pat and Larry, owners of Acme Welding.

Larry & Beverly

Pat & Mary Allen

Originally designed to be more conventional, I came up with an idea to build a fold down side to use as a serving line during one of my visits to Acme to check on the progress...Larry and Pat walked away shaking their heads in disbelief. They thought I was insane.

I coaxed them back and after a long conversation said, "I know you can do it, you're the best." They accepted my challenge, doubtful it could be done, but willing to do their best. The designing and drafting happened prior to computers and AutoCAD. These geniuses prevailed and today our 20-foot showstopper "Grand Daddy" boasts a side that folds down electrically and becomes a full serving line.

It has a 1,000 pound capacity rotisserie, a 30-gallon steam kettle, a sink, a 100-gallon fresh water system with holding tanks to meet health codes, a griddle, a 20-foot hot and cold serving line and a pantry for keeping dry goods. Since 1992 "Grand Daddy's" record setting feat of serving 1,000 people per hour stands firm, making it the king of our fleet.

I'm happy to report, after all the postponed anniversary dinners, I have the most understanding wife in the world. All is still well in our household and we will be celebrating 50/70 this year. That means fifty years of marriage and my 70th birthday. We've made many memories and acquired thousands of friends on the road to becoming the cooking team we are today.

The demand for our services continued to grow and we added more charities along the way. Each year Horacene and I covered most of the operating expenses out of our own pockets. As the volunteer team grew, we continued building pits, grills and adding trailers so the cooking equipment can be towed to the events where we are cooking food. Eventually, we outgrew our facility and our budget. We realized we'd have to bring in more money to cover the operating expenses for LTC and continue serving the community.

Our first attempt at raising money was unsuccessful. We applied for a 10,000 dollar grant with a local refinery. When their board met, some board members favored a cooking team that participated in barbecue cook offs. We lost out on that one.

It was a bitter, but valuable experience. We realized to grow, our name had to be changed from "Cooking Team" to "Charity Team" to reflect what we actually do. For us that means no cook-offs or catering. There's nothing wrong with cook-offs. However, we figured most of our sponsors don't want to see their money spent on a good time, without all our efforts directed to charitable causes.

That taught us the value of understanding the importance of a name. So, we finally changed our name from the Lighthouse Cooking Team to the Lighthouse Charity Team.

After this first failed attempt at raising money, we changed our tactics regarding funding. We didn't want to depend upon government funding due to the time it usually takes to get money up front or get reimbursed for expenses on the back end. So we:

- Applied for a 501(C) 3 designation. This allows sponsors to write donations off on their taxes.
- Invested 4,000 dollars to hire a grant writer to prepare grant requests we could submit to private donors.
- Reached out to individuals we knew would be interested in our mission.
- Contacted business owners in the community.

We knew people in our local community would like to see where any money they donated was going instead of writing a check and never knowing how it was used.

Now that our decisions on how to fund the organization were made, we turned to the issue of deciding where our rapidly growing organization should be housed.

Our first building, known as FOC (Friendswood Operation Center), was built in 1988 and was attached to our residence. We intended to use this 4,000 square foot addition, which housed a 20-foot by 40-foot kitchen and two large bays for trailer storage, for another fifteen years until I retired at age fifty. I thought then I would use it to store a motorhome and a boat.

Well, as things go, time passed and Horacene and I continued having fun helping others. So, while we did eventually buy a motorhome, the idea of retiring and taking it on a cross-country trip didn't happen until many years later. Instead, in 1999 we built another building on our property, adding an additional 7,500 square feet of storage space for the organization. Scott Gordon started in 1990 working in my Insurance Agency.

His job description also included duties with the LCT. The Team was a large part of his life. Scott and his wife Heather eventually bought the property adjacent to ours and built a home for their family.

Scott was like a son to us and we were thrilled. We felt this demonstrated his commitment to the LCT. He and his wife Heather were able to become more involved in the day-to-day operation in preparation for Scott's future leadership role in the organization. He began handling the operations of the LCT when Horacene and I went out of town.

A Major Setback – the Building Fire

At this point we thought we were set, but fate had another plan. In 2001, as Horacene lay in a hospital bed recovering from minor surgery and watching the news on TV, she was horrified to see our Friendswood Operation Center building on fire. "It was like a bad dream," she remembers. "I lay there seeing everything we'd worked for engulfed in flames while I watched helplessly from my hospital bed. It was awful."

**"Stage Daddy" was a state of the art mobile sound stage used as the
entertainment venue during events and was lost in the fire
and never replaced.**

I left the hospital in the evening after visiting hours ended and
went to bed. I woke up when I heard our cat crying at the bed-
room door. When I looked outside I was shocked to see fire coming through the roof of our building. Scott had already called the
Fire Department and, even though they arrived in minutes, it was
too late to save anything.

Ultimately the fire destroyed our largest building, over 7,500
square feet housing most of our equipment. Trailers, trucks and
cooking equipment, it was a total loss and we were devastated.
All that hard work over the years and in a flash everything was
gone.

"We shed tears and thought our future with the LCT was over," remembers Horacene.

The next morning I went to pick up Horacene from the hospital. On the drive home, in shock, we discussed how we should proceed. Honestly, we were depressed. The thought of what it would take to rebuild was daunting. We thought maybe this was a sign it was time to give it all up and retire. We could take the insurance money, buy that motorhome and boat and finally take off to see the country.

No sooner did we enter our house when we heard a knock on our door. It was Scott, Tim Miller of Equusearch, and a group of our volunteers.

"We've come to start the cleanup and get this operation back on its feet," they said. A short while later, still reeling from the loss, Ross Benson with Benson Pipeline delivered track hoes with roll off dumpsters. He began crushing the trailers, putting them in dumpsters to be hauled off to the local dump.

When the building was emptied, our Fire Department returned with a pumper and washed out the building. Hundreds of local residents came by or called asking us, "What will you do now? Is this the end of LCT? What can we do to help?"

How could we not rebuild with that kind of dedicated, caring community support? The tipping point came when the local City Council and the Mayor came over and asked if they could help us acquire a building permit.

Horacene and I realized we had to rebuild. We looked resignedly at Scott and he knew we were asking him to join the rebuilding effort. Without a word, he agreed. In typical LCT manner, while he was procuring the permit to rebuild, he asked if we could build it "a little bigger." He figured if you don't ask, you won't receive.

We all kicked into high gear, gathered volunteers, acquired donations and sponsors to help with the rebuild and oversee the entire project, no small feat.

Six months and thousands of volunteer hours later, the new building was ready. It housed the trailers and gear, fabrication shop and tools. The rebuilt trailers were custom designed to meet our specific needs. By now we knew what worked and what didn't work. The frames, axel, electrical and plumbing were crafted to the highest standards.

The steel structure for the new building arrived on two trailers.

We used stainless steel and top grade paint, heavy duty hardware and commercial grade restaurant equipment because we know the kind of wear and tear the gear gets when cooking thousands of pounds of food and serving thousands of people per day. The new equipment would allow us to maintain fine restaurant standards even though we're all on wheels, totally mobile. The Open House party was a proud moment for our volunteers, the entire community, and us.

A Second Location for the LCT

Horacene and I lost our prized custom built motorhome in the fire. Shortly thereafter, we purchased another motorhome. With no place to store it, we moved it to an RV Park in Galveston. We purchased a vacant property and built a weekend residence on it.

One Sunday in 2002, as we were leaving church, our Priest said, "I know who you are. Would you be interested in cooking for our church festival?"

That was the start of LCT's involvement in Galveston, an island community 25 miles south of Friendswood. Once again, using our weekend residence as the new Galveston location, we towed trailers and equipment to the Island site we called "The Landing" on an as needed basis.

Our new volunteers on the Island were mostly retirees, which we affectionately called GGG's, or "The Galveston Geriatric Group." Today, we refer to them as the "Galveston Good Guys" in honor of all they do. You can see from the picture below they "See, Speak and Hear" no evil.

Larry Mignerey, Leo Ritzler, Kenny Wegner

A Time of Miracles

We cooked at this location from 2002 until 2011, as we continued building a reputation for helping others. In the meantime, we developed a relationship with Larry Del Papa, owner of Anheuser-Busch's Galveston Distributorship known as Del Papa Distributing. Larry, an astute businessman, had outgrown his former Galveston location and built a new state of the art facility just outside Galveston. His outgrown facility was put up for sale or lease.

In an incredible gesture of kindness and generosity, Larry, a third generation Galvestonian donated the use of his former and now unused building to the Lighthouse Charity Team. He knew the difference the LCT made and would continue making to the Island. It set off a chain of what we called "miracles." *This was the first.* In 2011 we proudly opened our second Lighthouse Charity Team location now known as the GOC, or Galveston Operations Center. Not only is this 22,000 square foot building fully air conditioned, it's equipped with offices and a meeting room that holds up to 75 people along with a warehouse and shop space for equipment upgrades and repairs. It was an opportunity to help expand our operation and we gratefully accepted

Military vets Steve Comstock, Larry Spurgeon, Leo Ritzler, Frank Provinziano, Kenny Wegner, Dave Gillioz

We had an Open House for five days, since we could only accommodate 300 per evening. Each night was a different invited group: Team Members, Chamber of Commerce Members, Emergency Response, Businesspersons in the Community, and finally the General Public throughout the day. The Galveston Restaurant Association donated and served all of the food. Del Papa and Glazier Foods, the beverages.

**Larry & Joan Del Papa, Daugirds, JoAnn & Lawrence Del Papa
dedicating the use of the building to the Team.**

Dick & Lawrence share one of Lawrence's favorite beverages. The Budweiser® "Red & White" he claimed made their company famous.

We built a prep kitchen to initially allow us work from this former warehouse.

As we considered the cost of retrofitting the building for our needs, we had no idea where the money would come from. We wanted to install two commercial kitchens to house a 1,000 pound capacity rotisserie barbecue pit, convection ovens, tilt braising pans, a flat top grill, fryers and a Halon system not to mention a meeting room for weekly volunteer briefings. It would take a large investment. We had volunteers with the expertise to do the work, now we just needed the money.

Here came Miracle Number Two: Our prayers were answered when Boyd Yarbrough, another generous donor, immediately saw he could help by donating a 30,000 dollar rotisserie toward the retrofit of the newly acquired building.

Miracle Number Three followed. Shortly thereafter, Hector Villar-real of CVA Houston called Scott out of the blue. "Scott," he said, "I'm closing a restaurant. If I sell all the equipment, I'm told I can only get twenty cents on the dollar. I figure it's better to give you the equipment where it can do some good. So, if you want it, it's yours, come and haul it off."

Scott, never one to let any grass grow under his feet, tore out to inspect the equipment to ensure it was worthy of taking. He called Hector and said, "I'm on my way."

Hector responded he would leave keys and alarm code at his house if Scott wanted to come by and get them. Scott gladly drove fifty miles to Hector's, then another fifty miles back to the restaurant. He was delighted to discover the equipment looked brand new. In fact, he discovered the equipment was less than eighteen months old. When Hector closed the restaurant he lit-erally walked out, locked the doors and left.

The storage room as it existed when we moved in the building.

This photograph shows the total retrofit of this room to a health approved $300,000 commercial kitchen.

Miracle Number Four occurred next. We had requested a $75,000 grant from the Moody Memorial First United Methodist Church Personal Endowment Fund and we got word it was approved. When good things happen God certainly sends a powerful message. We immediately began the renovation process on the former Del Papa building, and our loyal, dedicated volunteer team members performed all the work.

Ribbon cutting for new kitchen with Grant from Moody

Miracle Number Five came rolling in. The lighting in the building included outdated Halogen lights that are not only expensive to run but they emit a lot of heat. As a result our cooling bill skyrocketed. We needed cooler running, more energy efficient LED fixtures. One day a friend came by the new building to assess our needs and see what he could do to help. His quote for replacing all the lights in the 22,000 square foot building was a hefty 35,000 dollars. When he asked me about our budget, I sheepishly told him, "All we have is 5,000 dollars budgeted to replace the lights."

He thanked me and left. I thought it was over. Two weeks later, he called me back and said, "Dick, if you still have that five grand, I'll bring the lights to you and your licensed volunteer electricians can install them." Another prayer was answered.

The Results: Our Fleet and Capability

Each of our trailers is designed to fulfill a specific purpose. From:

- "Big Daddy," which cooked over 100,000 pounds of meat last year to
- "Craw Daddy", capable of cooking 1,500 of shrimp at a time, to
- "Grand Daddy" with a serving line capable of serving 1,000 meals per hour. We now have 15 state of the art trailers.

We can serve any dish from fajitas to T-bone steak. We cook chili, spaghetti, Mexican fare or scrambled eggs and bacon. We bake potatoes, and roast corn on the cob, but my favorite is the Lighthouse rib eye with mushrooms. We make gallons of our own barbecue sauce and have a special refrigeration unit for soft drinks, water and iced tea. When our team members aren't welding sheet metal or twirling wrenches, they pride themselves on their culinary talent. They're good at it, get lots of practice and they love helping out any way they can.

To date our organization has raised over 20 million dollars for other non-profits and has served over one million meals. The LCT helps raise money for all types of charities including schools, churches, scout troops, little league teams, emergency responders, military servicemen, veterans, Blue Santa Toys for kids, service organizations, fundraisers for children and adults battling terminal illnesses, victims of natural disasters such as hurricanes, tornadoes, floods, and fires, and aids in searches for missing persons.

I am fortunate enough to have a capable successor. I've turned the reins over to Scott Gordon. As for Horacene and I, we finally get to take our long overdue motorhome journey around the country. He is Vice President of Operations and came to us when he was just eighteen years old. He's always treated us as if we were his parents. I was the best man at his wedding twenty years ago.

R-Wallace Trochesset, Sheriff Henry's brother, also a great cook, Team Member and Sponsor.

He's grown to be like a son to us. He, his wife Heather and son Cole have made many sacrifices to make the organization what it is today. They're fiercely loyal to the Team and he'll be the per- fect person to take over when Horacene and I finally retire.

Capable of doing it all, Scott's adept at speaking to audiences as well as the news media. Team members respect him for his leadership, organizational and teaching skills. He knows how to raise funds and always deals with our sponsors in a professional manner. Horacene and I are extremely proud of Scott and the businessman, husband and father he's become as we've watched him grow from a teen to a man.

The Lighthouse Charity Team will continue as part of our legacy long after we're no longer physically able to help or finally depart this planet. It's part of our plan. As the old saying goes, "None of us are going to get out of here alive!"

Scott, pictured with co-author of this book Lorraine Grubbs at the Waterford Yacht Club Regatta.

Chapter Two

The First Ingredient - Leadership

Whether you're in charge of a small business, a Fortune 500 corporation or a rag-tag group of volunteers with good intentions in their heart who want to serve and help, leadership is essential. In this chapter we'll dive into how great leadership makes a difference. Co-author Lorraine Grubbs is a Management Consultant who played a pivotal role leading at Southwest Airlines for many years. She shares her insights here including twelve ways in which great leaders like Dick excel.

At the head of any great organization, you'll find a great leader. Like Southwest's illustrious former leader, Herb Kelleher, Dick's similar approach to people is uncanny. Both leaders possess a unique way of putting people immediately at ease. With a warm hug he'll say to someone new, "I'm so glad to meet you." Both men make you feel like you're the most important person in the room. Those are close to the exact words I heard from each upon meeting them, the first as a new hire and the second as a new volunteer. Though they lead very different groups, one of employees and the other volunteers, they have a great deal in common.

Here are the twelve leadership principles Dick lives by:
1) Treat people as equals. It doesn't matter what you've accomplished in life, Dick treats you as an equal. As a result, people feel valued and respected from the onset.

2) Become an excellent listener. Dick's total attention is on you when you speak and he actually remembers what you say. When you meet him later he'll bring up something you said in your previous conversation.

3) Give praise and thanks frequently. Dick never toots his own horn, though there are multiple reasons why he could. Try to commend him for something he did and he'll immediately turn it around, giving credit to others. Dick says, "I'd rather thank people more times than necessary because we simply couldn't be as effective without them."

4) Notice what's going on around you. When Dick sees someone alone, he'll bring them into the fold and include them. As a volunteer this is important because people need and want to feel included. Volunteers have a choice of where they want to spend their time. This honors their choice of choosing your organization.

5) Makes sacrifices for the organization. Over the years Dick and Horacene have invested their own savings in Lighthouse Charities multiple times when needed.

6) Trust in people. Dick delegates authority and builds up the confidence of others. New people learning a business will inevitably make mistakes, so forgive and move on. Dick says, "Volunteers don't make mistakes. They can't be fired. If something goes wrong, we can correct it so we don't worry about it." This allows volunteers to feel trusted and they'll be more apt to take risks and make decisions when necessary.

7) Communicate effectively with people. This is especially vital when delivering a tough message. Dick says "I can lower the boom in a nice way. I tell people I'm here to help them, not tear them down. I want you to see what I'm seeing and hopefully, you'll agree. If not, show me a reason why I'm wrong."

8) Lead your organization like a family. Dick's nickname is "Big Daddy," adopted by the LCT volunteers and the nickname was later used to name their biggest cooking trailer. He treats his people like *family* and if talk to any of the volunteers, they would agree they indeed are a *family*.

9) Create a successful, unique business model. LCT was founded on the concept of helping charities raise money. Dick states, "We've traveled America and have never seen an organization like ours. We've never talked to anyone who claims to be as active or give back as much. We have unique equipment including custom trailers and trucks. We can raise as much as a half a million dollars in an evening. We're not in debt, everything is paid for."

10) Always lead through love. Dick uses the word "love" freely around the LCT. He wants his family of hundreds of volunteers to feel cared for and he personally will tell them he "loves them" when they're together. You can tell he's sincere and he means it.

11) Learn to be a people person. Dick's wife Horacene states, "Dick is a real people person. He knows how to uplift them, make them feel his equal and make them feel proud. It's a special knack he has. He never talks down to people. He talks to them on their level. He never throws his weight around and uses a soft touch. People like following him because he has a sense of leadership. He knows what needs to be done."

12) Be unflappable – which means calm under fire. Dick is touted to be a great crisis manager. "Things simply don't ruffle his feathers," Horacene says. "If someone comes to him with a question, he usually has an answer. If he doesn't, he knows who to contact to get the answer. He's a good problem solver."

Many experts suggest the best way to lead is by example. Perhaps in your career or charitable work you've observed a leader who embodies some or all of the twelve characteristics, qualities and attributes listed above. You might choose to take on one of these characteristics and see how it makes a difference with the people you lead. Once you feel comfortable in your own skin incorporating this new attitude or behavior, how about taking on another attribute listed above?

You'll discover your leadership quotient will improve and it'll be easier bringing people around to your way of thinking and naturally respond to your requests with enthusiasm. Try it. I'm sure you'll be pleased with the results.

Chapter Three

The Second Ingredient - Volunteers

*"People who have time make excuses,
people who don't have time, make the time."*

Judge Robert F. B. (Skip) Morse

Preparing, cooking and serving food is work. Don't forget the clean up afterward, too. Multiply that times hundreds or even thousands of hungry people at an event and you've got hot, back-straining, energy-draining work. However, our LCT volunteers and sponsors tell us the smiles and sense of satisfaction that comes from helping others who need help brings them a deep sense of purpose and joy.

Since charitable organizations can't dole out salaries, attracting and keeping volunteers willing to go the extra mile is critical to achieving your goals. In this chapter, Lorraine will dive into the mystery to LCT's loyal volunteers and sponsors. In our Resource Guide you'll also find easy tips to help you find the kind of people who'll help your organization grow as a respected part of the community and a source of local pride.

People who volunteer aren't in it for the money. Helping others is their motivation.

There's no one better than Dick Daugird to explain some of his experiences over the last two decades with volunteers himself. Then, in the interest of equality, we thought it was a good idea to let some volunteers speak for themselves in the next three chapters.

In the LCT organization, it's considered an honor to be recognized as a Team Leader for a project. LCT bestows their "Gray Hat" designation on deserving volunteers and they proudly take charge of the event.

Gray Hat team leaders are in charge of operations for an entire event from ordering food and getting the equipment ready to cooking, delivering everything to the site, serving the food, returning the equipment to the Operations Center and cleaning it, then entering it back into inventory so it is ready to go for the next event.

They trust their people and treat them like family. They know they can count on Dick and count on each other for whatever needs to be done. Much of their motivation comes from community recognition. Team Members enjoy the recognition and pride of belonging to a well-respected organization. Their pride is reinforced by the comments and compliments they hear from people throughout the community.

Lorraine remembers her experience at Southwest Airlines and how the pride Dick refers to above translated to employees.

I remember as a Southwest Airlines employee, walking into the grocery store in my uniform. People would literally stop me to tell me how much they loved Southwest and then share their favorite Southwest Airlines story.

It takes more than just enthusiasm. Leading volunteers, as Lorraine explains from her book "How to Create a Happy Workplace" means making the environment fun, delegating responsibility and much more.

An organization is only as good as its people. The Lighthouse Charity Team includes about three hundred loyal volunteers. As a group they dedicate over 25,000 hours of their own personal time annually and range in age from teens to senior citizens.

Most help the Lighthouse Charity Team on a regular basis at both the Galveston and Friendswood locations. During an average one year period, LCT volunteers complete eighty events and serve an incredible fifty thousand people.

What's the secret to their dedication? After all, LCT volunteers don't draw paychecks. Lifting, cooking over a hot grill, serving, sweating and repairing equipment is not exactly easy. Yet, they continuously show up to work.

What's LCT's secret sauce? It's no different than Lorraine's four *Guiding Beacons*, described below, she uses to help business leaders in creating a Happy Workplace where the "one thing" is Putting People First. She describes how the four Guiding Beacons are alive and well at LCT.

1) Recruit for Attitude, Train for Skill. Attract the right types of people through building a reputation of excellence. LCT volunteers are recruited by current volunteers or people recommended through the community. Dick states, "When I visit with someone interested in joining our team, I go with my gut. I'll give almost anyone a chance to work with us if I feel they're genuine. Above all, we look for people with an attitude of service."

2) Motivate volunteers by creating the right atmosphere. Make work fun. The LCT volunteers take their job seriously, but take themselves lightly. While working an event, people tell jokes, play practical jokes on each other and laugh a lot.

In the corporate world motivating employees with bonuses or monetary rewards for a job well done is typical. Due to IRS restrictions in the not-for-profit environment, awards considered to have a monetary value aren't permitted. So, it's more important than ever to ensure you continuously thank people with a pat on the back or encouraging word. The LCT is dedicated to letting people know their contributions are truly valued.

3) Lead with Service. As mentioned earlier, having a heart to serve starts from the top.

Lighthouse Charity Team Leaders motivate volunteers in the following ways:

- They get to know volunteers by working right alongside them.

- They don't ask a volunteer to do something they haven't already done or would be unwilling to do themselves.

- They delegate authority which shows the volunteers respect and trust.

- They are all equals. There is no rank order; rather they believe everyone is equal and able to take charge of whatever is needed.

4) Create a Sense of Ownership. Volunteers of Lighthouse Charity Team know the mission of the organization you read at the beginning of this book. They know it is to acquire and prepare the food and provide volunteer labor at no cost to their fundraising partners.

The communication channels at LCT are crystal clear. People know what's going on, LCT's purpose and how they fit in the bigger picture. They feel connected and aware of what's going on within the organization through their weekly group meetings.

Dicks explains, "Regular meetings are critical for two reasons. First, it gets everyone on the same page. Second, it keeps people connected. Even if you don't have meeting space, find ways to meet at someone's house, in their garage, at a local chamber office, a church hall or another meeting room in the community. At LCT we meet every Monday in Friendswood and on Tuesdays in Galveston, except on holidays. Whatever day you choose keep it consistent.

Board meetings are held at 4:00 p.m. Usually 12–18 team members attend. The advisory board meeting is open to all team members who wish to discuss event requests and other business topics as deemed necessary. They also sometimes handle sensitive issues not relevant to the larger group.

The general group meeting is held after the board meeting from 5:00-6:00 p.m. After the meeting wraps up, dinner prepared by our volunteers is served. A donation of five dollars is standard to cover the cost of the food, but we don't necessarily enforce that guideline. We make a special point of inviting new members. The general meetings review the previous week's events, plan future events and occasionally hear from guest speakers about topics of interest. At any general meeting they may hear from leaders like Bill Read, the former director of the National Hurricane Center, or motivational speakers like Lorraine, who provides tips and ideas on how to better their teamwork skills through her "Lessons in Loyalty" message."

"When a new volunteer joins, if they stay more than one year, and eighty-five percent of ours do, they're committed," states Dick. "Within that critical first year, they build friendships and work many of the positions. They come to understand what we do and where their expertise can contribute most. Whether it's purchasing food, preparing for events, equipment clean up, photography, or lending a hand with maintenance; once they find their niche, many stay over a decade. We encourage them to attend our weekly meetings telling them, "We'll be talking about you and you need to be present to defend yourself. If you miss a meeting, you may get volunteered for something.""

Many charities struggle with recruitment of volunteers. LCT has never had that issue. One secret they use to add volunteers is by asking the host charity for a few of their people to help with a joint event. When their volunteers show up, the team gives them a quick lesson on how to cook and serve. This helps two ways:

- First, it ensures they have adequate coverage for each event.

- Second, it connects them to a community they may not know as people see familiar local faces serving the food.

They also partner with the local Sheriff Department to utilize volunteers who need to fulfill community service requirements. These volunteers come from two sources. The first are sent by local judges. They're people with traffic fines who don't have the money to pay. They're usually mandated to complete fifteen hours of community service and are happy to work inside a building rather than on the side of a freeway.

The second group is offenders from the jail escorted by a deputy to perform cleaning tasks or move equipment. Dick shares, "We had an inmate who was an experienced floor tile guy and he was going to install a new floor in our kitchen. On Monday, he called Gordon Morse, a retired Galveston P.D. Officer and told him the Judge dismissed him to return to work. He was on the front steps of the jail with no ride or money. Gordon agreed to pick him up, buy him some toiletries, clothing and a room for the week at Motel 6. The next morning he started laying the floor for our new kitchen. He did an excellent job. The floor is beautiful and he completed it in only five days saving us thousands of dollars. We ended up paying him a reasonable daily rate, which helped him get back on his feet. It was a good deal for all concerned."

Volunteers, founders and officers of LCT aren't paid. The LCT employs four people who are available to accept deliveries and perform building and equipment maintenance. Dick clarifies, "In the event of a last minute crisis, such as broken trailer lights, a flat tire, a refrigeration problem or something else they can be counted on to rectify the problem.

When the equipment is returned to our site, they're responsible for making sure everything's working again. For an operation the size of our charity, the payroll is extremely small. We joke that our toilet paper bill exceeds our payroll."

"We try to make volunteering meaningful and fun," states Dick. "Once a friend came by to check out the operation and confessed they didn't know how to volunteer. We put him on the serving line all day. He later said, "I never knew volunteering could be so much fun." He became a loyal member of our team.

It's easy to get hooked on volunteering at LCT. People with empty stomachs tend to praise and compliment others. Nothing will take your mind off stress in your life like serving people who are less fortunate. It's a way to mingle with existing and new friends before everyone goes their separate way for the week."

Just because you run a non-profit doesn't mean you shouldn't have metrics like a business. To measure the effectiveness of volunteers, use statistics like hours served and the value in dollars, of a volunteer's time. Lighthouse Charity Team tracks volunteer hours to understand and improve efficiency.

Chapter Four

In Our Volunteers' Own Words

Ross McClintock, Volunteer since 1996

I was introduced to LCT in 1996 through the Boy Scouts. The organization was helping my son's troop raise funds by cooking and selling fajita dinners. As we were delivering the meals in Styrofoam containers, a big guy walked up and introduced himself as Dick Daugird. He peppered me with questions about who I was and where I was from, so we started a friendly conversation.

I knew what he was doing. As any good charitable promoter, I figured he was looking for me to volunteer or become a sponsor with the LCT.

"What do you do," he asked?

"I'm in the electrical business," I responded.

"You know what?" Dick said, "I need some extension cords." Well, when he says extension cords, it brings to mind the little orange things sold at Home Depot. I buy them by the case, and Home Depot buys them by the train carload. I figured I could give them to him at my cost and they'd still be more expensive than he could get them elsewhere.

So, I was honest. I said, "Dick, if I were you, I'd just go to Home Depot." He looked at me like I just ran over his puppy so I asked, "Dick, What am I missing?"

He replied, "Let me show you." Then he walked me over to his equipment. I clearly saw the operation was bigger than the "mom and pop charity."

I envisioned as I noticed the size of one of theirs trailer loaded with cooking equipment. I thought, "this is a commercial establishment."

Dick pointed to the extension cord and I realized he was referring to a portable power cord.

The thing looked the size of something Barnum & Bailey or Exxon would use. It was huge! "Dick," I said, "This isn't an extension cord, it's a portable power cord."

"Well I need them," he replied.

"You know what?" I said. "I've got about ten thousand feet of those in my warehouse. I can also see you need a lot of other things around here. Seems like some things were just thrown together. Some of it's safe, some of it is unsafe. When's your next event?"

"We have an event next week," Dick said. I found myself saying, "Let me come over on Wednesday. I'll bring a catalog with me and we'll figure out what you need. Before your event next week,

I'll make sure you have stuff that's the correct size, and ensure it's installed safely."

"Great," said Dick.

As I walked away that day I thought, "How'd he do that? How'd he pull me in and get me involved?" That's when I realized, the magic of Dick Daugird. Over the years, I even inherited a nick-name I don't cherish, but it stuck… The Electrical Fairy.

My daughter and son-in-law are now involved with LCT. As a medical student finishing up her degree and with his project en-gineer background, they're as committed to the organization as I am. *People Helping People*.

Rob Fee of Plylox, Volunteer since 1989

I started working with the LCT in 1989. I had friends who were volunteering and they loved the organization, so I decided to see what it was all about.

I hadn't started my own company yet. I was working in the oil fields, raising three kids and my paycheck barely stretched to cover our living expenses. Each time we'd come volunteer for these events Dick would take a big pan full of leftovers and di-vide it up among the volunteers. We'd bring it home and we'd eat the leftovers for a couple days. It was nice having the extra food.

Over the years Dick showed us over and over how much he cared. He was always taking care of the volunteers.

One of the most memorable events I have as a LCT member happened in January of 1986 when I got a call from Scott asking me to rush over to Kroger where I bought enough food to fill the entire truck bed of my pickup. We were headed to Nacogdoches to feed the first responders investigating the fatal crash of NASA's space shuttle Challenger. It was intense and we worked long and hard. I truly learned how LCT could impact the lives of the community in a positive way despite tough situations. *People Helping People*.

Kitten Brizendine, Volunteer since 1984

My introduction to the LCT was through the Friendswood community. As a member of the City Council, I attended many local civic events such as the Fourth of July parade, American Heart

Association dinners, etc. I often saw Dick, Horacene and volunteers cooking and serving folks at these events. One day a friend of mine invited me to an LCT event she was volunteering for, so I went. Meeting Dick, Horacene and the Team, I realized they were doing something worthwhile and special, so I decided to join them.

A few months later we got the opportunity to participate in the Jerry Lewis Muscular Dystrophy Association (MDA) fundraising event held at the Lighthouse location. I jumped in with both feet. Knowing Dick and the Team would be cooking; I wanted to add an element of entertainment to the event. So, I appointed myself the "Entertainment Coordinator" for that event and went to work.

Throughout my years on the City Council, I made quite a few contacts within our community. I got in touch with the schools to help with the MDA event and arranged drill teams and dancers to entertain. This was a win/win because it drew the parents who wanted to see their children perform. We also added tours of the Lighthouse and music provided by a local disc jockey.

The first event was so successful we repeated it for another seven years. Each year I added new touches of entertainment. We had car shows, air shows, live bands, fast-draw gun competitions, hot air balloon demonstrations and petting zoos.

Channel 2, KPRC, heard about the event and came out to do live interviews at our site. We even found a way to televise our live auction over the airwaves. (We won't disclose the volunteer who scaled the tower and plugged into the satellite dish). It was so much fun. We became the largest MDA pledge center for the Galveston/Houston area.

Eventually, we were so successful the event outgrew the Lighthouse location and the MDA moved to a larger venue. But the years we were involved were amazing ones. The memories created by those annual events became a highlight in this self-appointed "Entertainment Coordinator's" life.

Thank you, LCT for letting me make a positive difference. I will forever be grateful.

James Besch Volunteer/Sponsor since 1998

The teamwork you'll find throughout LCT is remarkable. It all starts with the heart. Everyone here has a big heart. Our Team Members are dedicated to the mission. It's common to hear someone shout out, "Hey, we've got a storm coming, let's get this done!"

Everyone chips in and the left hand knows what the right hand is doing. Whether working on an event for the community or one of our own, we jump in and get it done.

We've cooked twelve thousand pounds of crawfish and five thousand pounds of chicken in a single day. Because of the Team's commitment we do more with a small group of volunteers than I ever thought possible.

I'm retired and can't imagine who else I would drive one hundred miles round trip up to four times a week to help. It's about the camaraderie and fun along with the work.

We all have something we bring and contribute – electricians, air conditioning specialists, cooking and maintenance experts…you name it and we've got it.

Sometimes new volunteers join and say, "I can't do anything." Our team will point them a certain direction and train them. They build them up and make them feel important. Whether it's putting an ad in the paper or tackling a plumbing problem, they'll teach you. We never hesitate to share our talent and knowledge. In turn, we ask you pay it forward and share it with other new volunteers when they come on board.

I like to make things happen so I enjoy working with the team because we make things happen.

Scott called me one day and said, "I need your help. I'm not sure if it's for a day or five weeks, but we need you."

I simply replied, "Okay."

Kelly Childress, Volunteer and Sponsor since 1995

I was working at a fabrication shop in La Porte when a friend of mine asked me to drive to Ramsey Prison to meet Dick Daugird and Scott Gordon. They were organizing a fundraising event to help a home for abused women and children. It was supposed to be held the next day in the fields behind the prison.

After visiting with them awhile, Dick asked, "Do you want to come out tomorrow?"

I said, "Sure. You don't mind if I bring my wife, do you? She's pregnant and I don't want to leave her alone."

"Bring her!" said Dick's wife, Horacene.

The next day my wife and I drove out and jumped in to help the team. People were genuine and friendly. We were hooked.

That was 21 years ago. I've stayed due to the camaraderie and the mission of *People Helping People*. I enjoy doing it. I'm not a person who enjoys the limelight. I don't do this for recognition. I like to come out and say, "Hey, let me help you out," do my job and leave. I enjoy helping people.

I feel my biggest contribution to the organization is my expertise helping to build the trailers. I don't have a college degree, but I have a lot of mechanical knowledge. You might call it common sense. When I started with the cooking team we had four trailers. We have eighteen now. I've had a hand in building the majority of them.

Steve and Debra Pease Broom Volunteers since 2011

I retired and started looking around for something to do. I'd heard about Lighthouse Charities through my insurance agent, Scott. My church was having an event and needed twenty briskets. I called Scott to ask if they could cook the briskets for us.

He said, "Sure, come on."

I didn't know anything about the organization or the equipment they owned. When we dropped the briskets off, we toured the facility and met some of the volunteers. We liked the atmosphere and were intrigued with their business model.

Once Lighthouse approves your fundraising the event, they arrange to provide the food, which costs three dollars per person. The meals are sold at the event for fifteen dollars a plate, allowing the receiving organization to keep twelve dollars for their fundraising efforts.

That's a whopping 80 percent return on investment. It was a great model and we really liked what they were doing. Slowly we got more involved. When Debra retired, we both made this our full time mission.

We worked our way up from dishwashers to cookers. Now we're Gray Hatters, in charge of events. Why do we do it? Because we see the benefit. For example, we went to a dig site that was being overseen by Texas Equusearch. Dig sites are tough assignments because rescuers are looking for bodies, usually those of abducted children. We provided some relief from this tough duty. FBI agents, Texas Rangers and Friendswood Police were all there. A gruesome task was made just a tad easier with our hot food and friendly smiles. We heard statements like, "We're not giving up until we find them."

"Well," we responded, "We'll be right here with you, no matter how long it takes, don't you worry." In one case, we ended up staying for weeks. It took a little creativity to vary up the menu. We took turns cooking our favorite grandmothers' recipes and ended up with great lasagna, jambalaya etc.

From those who provide shelter to abused women, church groups honoring their pastor, or the Galveston County Rodeo, our cooking team shows up with smiles and positive energy to help. We've served crowds ranging in size from fifty people to five thousand, it's all part of the mission. We're there to make sure people have good, home cooked meals. We don't make one penny off the food.

In every event I've participated in it always feels like we touched someone or they touch us in a personal way.

I work full time with a major oil company, but dedicate another twenty hours per week to the LCT. For us it's a family thing. My wife and children volunteer, too. In fact my daughter baked the cake for this event today.

My sense of dedication came to me during the years I spent with the Marine Corps. They taught me you're not done until the job's done. They instilled in us a belief that there is no such thing as "above and beyond the call of duty." You have 5,000 people to feed, so jump in and get it done.

I have a great deal of respect for Dick and would do anything he asks. He's done so much for my family and me. When I was fresh out of the Marine Corps I got in a little trouble. Like a true friend he stood behind me and pulled me out. He and Horacene are awesome. Scott's followed in their footsteps and has a big heart, too.

Most of all, this organization lets me know the time I dedicate is worthwhile. I enjoy seeing the relief and smile on peoples' faces when we walk up and say, "We've got this covered. You don't have to worry about it."

Sandy and Don Gartman, Volunteers since 2014

As the former president of the Galveston Chamber of Commerce, Chairman of the Port of Galveston, and Chairman of the University of Houston Clear Lake Advisory Board, I'm deeply involved in the community of Galveston.

My wife and I met Dick when we got involved with Operation Blue Santa where police officers collect toys for families in need. Dick offered to house the more than six hundred bicycles we bought to give away that Christmas at his Galveston location.

Later, after touring the LCT's Galveston Operations Center, we were amazed at the amount of equipment they've amassed. When we finally attended our first meeting, we came to appreciate the whole team. We discovered how dedicated everyone is to both their cause and the community. These folks are the real thing. They have heart.

Family, Team, Fun. Those are the words I use to describe the organization's culture. The volunteers include people from all walks of life. The volume of work produced by the team is amazing, especially when you look at how they keep their costs down. Most charities take a large percentage of the money received and use it to fund their operations. Not so with Lighthouse Charity Team. Most of their money goes back into the community to help people.

The moment we attended our first meeting, Sandy and I felt like we were coming home. The meetings are amazingly efficient. They address all agenda items in a fast, decisive way and move on. The knowledge in that room is deep. On a whim, I once asked Scott if he knew what ingredients went into certain meals, and he quickly rattled them off.

Their good reputation has spread throughout the state of Texas. I'm not sure I should tell this story but one day I was driving to my ranch in south Texas and I was stopped for speeding. I had my Lighthouse shirt on and the officer asked, "Are you with the Lighthouse?"

"Yes sir," I responded.

"They do such a wonderful job. Slow down next time," he said and off he went.
My love of the people in the organization keeps me coming back. But my belief in the mission, *People Helping People,* keeps me inspired. Organizations like the LCT are the lifeblood of charity in our community. Anytime people have a tragedy in their life they can come to us, simply share their story, and, unless someone is trying to enrich themselves inappropriately, we help them.

After attending one of our meetings, I heard a visitor describe our group in this way, "Those people are so dedicated it's almost like a church group with beer."

I say, "Amen, brother!"

Roy Cizmar, Volunteer Since 1997

My neighbor approached me one day knowing I was in the air conditioning and refrigeration business. "I have a friend who does a little cooking," he said. "He's got a cooler on a trailer he's having trouble with. Would you mind looking at it?"

I replied, "Okay." He gave me Dick's number and I called him. He explained where they were and I said, "Yeah, I've seen a few trailers around there."
He replied, "Well if you'll come on over we can show you the problem.

I agreed and showed up, found the problem, fixed the cooler and was getting ready to walk out when I made a big mistake. I walked up to Dick and asked, "Have you got anything else broken?"

Dick furrowed his brow and said, "Well as a matter of fact, we have a trailer called 'Big Daddy'. It has a refrigerator no one seems to be able to fix."

Never one to back down from a challenge, I took a look at it, figured out the problem and told Dick I'd be back with parts in a week.

It was a couple weeks before Thanksgiving, and by the time I returned with the part, everyone was swarming around the trailer cooking turkeys like crazy. I had to work around all cooking activity to fix it, but I did. I've continued fixing things as part of the LCT for twenty years.

A few months later I saw my neighbor and said, "You know what? I don't know whether to shake your hand or hit you."

I've built good relationships with these folks and we've done many events together. We're a tight knit group and the camaraderie keeps us coming back. Dick and Scott always make people feel at home. "What do you need?" they ask. "How can we help you? We know you help the organization, so let us know what we can do for you."

My daughter had a tragic accident seven years ago. She was riding with her boyfriend in his car and they hit a cow. She ended up in a wheelchair as a quadriplegic. A lot of people kept telling me, "You need to do a fundraiser."

I said, "You know, we don't need it. We're okay."

They pushed and pushed until I finally said, "Okay, we're going to do it." With Scott's help we raised thirty thousand dollars.

We bought a piece of equipment that's helped a lot with her therapy. We've still got a little money in the account because we're conservative with it. She's doing well considering doctors told her she'd be on a respirator and never do anything physical again. Today she lives with her boyfriend who stayed beside her. She's never given up and keeps working hard to regain her mobility. She's taken about 45 steps on her own now. She even walked down the aisle at her sister's wedding with assistance.

Some of the most rewarding events LCT has done involve children. We've done fundraisers for kids with leukemia, for football players who got injured, for firemen who got burned, for the Boy Scouts and churches. It's all good stuff.

Here's an example how quickly we can pull things together. When the NASA Challenger shuttle exploded over east Texas back in 1986, I was sitting at the table having dinner with my in-laws and kids. It was a Saturday night. Scott called and said, "Hey, we got a call from the mayor of Friendswood asking if we'll go to Nacogdoches to help."

I said, "Okay, what are we going to do?"

He said, "We're going to go feed them."

I replied, "All right. When are we leaving?"

"Fast as we can get there," Scott answered.

Immediately I left the dinner table to meet Dick and the others. We started gathering everything we needed. Some went to Kroger buying every carton of eggs and package of bacon, everything we needed. We were determined to serve a hot breakfast the next morning, which was a Sunday. We loaded up, got the trailers hooked up and were on our way within four hours of getting the call.

A first responder came up to me and asked, "How many people can you feed? We have 80; can you handle it? Can you cook enough so everyone can have two tacos?"

I said, "You got nothing to worry about. We'll handle it." He didn't know we have the capacity to serve 5,000 people if needed, on four hours' notice.

Denise Stevenson, Volunteer since 2013 – Sponsor & Team Member

Denise generously donating one of two Kayaks to LCT

My son was an Engineering student at Texas A&M Galveston in 2013. He sent an email to LCT founder Dick Daugird. The email opened with "Howdy," which is a traditional A&M student greeting. He was a member of Engineers without Borders (EWB). The organization decided to undertake fundraising efforts to execute a project to bring clean water to a village in Nicaragua. This decision prompted the email to Dick requesting help with their first fundraising event.

Dick immediately responded and invited my son to come to a meeting to check out the LCT.

My son was impressed. From that point forward he started participating in events. A fundraiser was held for EWB, which funded the exploratory trip to Nicaragua. During the next year my son and his girlfriend, also a member of EWB, continued their volunteer efforts with LCT. They held a second fundraiser project, and another trip to Nicaragua was scheduled. During the second trip on my son's birthday, the digging process for the well to provide the village with clean water began. Four days later on his girlfriend's birthday, the digging was completed. The two-year effort was a huge success.

I called on the LCT to help with a fundraising shrimp boil for a local Civic Group in which I was involved. When I experienced the success of the event and the professionalism of the team, I started attending meetings. After seeing everything they were doing, I donated a jet-powered kayak to use as a raffle item for their yearly fundraiser.

The following year Lighthouse Charity Team did the Shrimp Boil Fundraiser event again. This time the funds were donated to them. I had so much confidence in the LCT I donated a second jet-powered kayak. I now attend meetings in both Galveston and Friendswood. I also volunteer as often as possible.

The awesome people involved with the LCT inspire the helping nature of us all to support people in need. It is my honor and privilege to be associated with Lighthouse Charity Team.

Norman and Debbie Frank, Volunteers since 2014

We discovered the LCT while helping with the Blue Santa Program in Galveston. Since Debbie and I enjoy helping others and meeting new people, the LCT was a perfect match for us and we're glad to help. Whether working a charitable event serving fifty or five thousand, we put forth the same effort to produce a professional result. The Lighthouse has become like a second family. Several immediate family members are also team members.

The first time we watched the history of the team on the LCT website video, it brought tears to our eyes. We feel blessed to be part of something that reaches out and help others in need. We all want to do something worthwhile to leave a mark. Through our volunteer work with LCT we fulfill that need.

Matt and Suzie Fleming, Volunteers since 1986

Matt and I have volunteered with Lighthouse Charity Team for more than 30 years now. Dick was our insurance agent and invited us. We liked the idea of being part of a group that supported local civic and charitable organizations.

We've stayed involved because the LCT continues making a difference in so many lives. Their unwavering commitment to serve the community by helping others creates a great feeling of being part of something bigger than us.

Matt says, "The first time I was invited to the Friendswood facility on Thanksgiving to fry turkeys, I was struck by the number of smoked turkeys to be distributed to people in need. It was an amazing demonstration of generosity."

Suzie says, "I was memorably welcomed to and thanked after participating in my first event. As we washed dishes, pots, pans, and utensils, we received genuine thanks for our time and effort."

Without LCT, we would've never been in the hangar at Ellington AFB to serve veterans and their families. We also would've never gone to Galveston after a hurricane to serve people in need. We've had the privilege to meet many first responders over the years.

The team displays genuine acts of kindness every day. There's a prevailing sense of caring, unselfishness and "cheering for success" in everything we do. Participating is fun. Matt and I even got the "count-on-able" award which means we can be counted on to respond to events when a call to action is made.

It gives us a sense of accomplishment knowing our small contributions make a difference. Following Dick, Horacene's, Scott's and Heather's lead is easy when you see their commitment. We feel we're part of the Lighthouse *family*. When the tables are turned and an LCT family member needs help with funerals, weddings, and other life events, they always show up with support.

Wallace Trochesset , volunteer since 2010

The LCT's generosity is overwhelming. There are few limits they will stop at to help others in need.

From feeding displaced families and first responders of local, state and national disasters, to helping a single family raise funds to offset medical bills to even purchasing a specially trained dog, they have done a lot.

Our family is blessed, so the LCT is great way to give back and help the less fortunate. We see what our compassionate help provides. Having that validation is nice. Working with everyone on the team over the years, we've built lifelong friendships. So we don't just work together, we play together as well. Going on vacation, attending Texan games, or just getting together for a good time, we enjoy each other's company.

The Lighthouse Charity Team should change their name to Lighthouse Charity *Family*. No matter what side of the serving line you're on they make you feel like you're family.

Dara Rychcik

My welcome to the team happened when I responded to an email my employer shared in which the LCT was soliciting volunteers to help during the aftermath of Hurricane Ike. I was put in touch with Suzie Fleming who needed help feeding first responders in Galveston. After work that day I made the heartbreaking drive down IH 45 to 61st street, seeing the devastation. Suzie introduced me to the group.

After the hugs and thanks I knew I found a group I wanted to help. I didn't feed people that night. I helped clean out a frozen food delivery truck. It was ninety degrees outside but freezing inside the truck. Despite my first effort, I was back again the next day, and the next.

Larry and Sherri Spurgeon, Volunteers since 2001 and 2003

Larry: Over fifteen years ago I heard about all the good work the LCT was doing. I decided to join them. I remember at one of my first events I was inspired by a young boy suffering from severe burns. Despite his pain, he still found a way to smile. I thought, "How on earth could I ever have a day as bad as that and yet he smiles?"

Through the LCT I feel I'm doing the Lord's work. The gratitude we get from those we help means more than a paycheck. Being around Dick, Scott and the team makes me want to be a better person. They're all like family to me.

Sherri says, "My husband Larry started volunteering with the LCT before I did. I occasionally went with him to the events and fell in love with the organization's mission. After I met Dick and Horacene, I was sold.

One of the first events I remember being involved in was a fundraiser for two brothers who were both firefighters with cancer. The event raised over $75,000 dollars in one night for them. The power of what we accomplished changed me forever as I realized how much of a difference we could make in the lives of others.

Last month both my husband and I volunteered over two hundred hours. Since 2003 I imagine we've put in at least 10,000 hours. We don't do it for recognition; we do it because we're *People Helping People*.

Ruthie Stayton, Volunteer since 2014

I had several friends who volunteered for the LCT and loved it. At their invitation I attended an event and that's all it took to convince me I wanted to be part of the team. When I showed up at my first team meeting, Gordon Morse was there. They told him I was a chef. He walked over to me, introduced himself and said, "You're a chef! Come see your new kitchen." They were without a chef since the previous one moved away. They had a beautiful new kitchen and I'm a sucker for a new kitchen.

I work full time as a real estate broker. I volunteer Monday afternoons and evenings to cook for the team during their weekly meetings. Leftovers are taken to the Tuesday meeting in Galveston. It's a win-win. I get to cook what I want and spend time with people who not only love to help, but love to eat. It's like a family and I love it.

Susan and Max Bowen, Volunteers and Sponsors since 1980

I was introduced to the LCT through my late husband Max Bowen who was a customer of Dick's insurance agency.

He donated the first barbecue to get them started and continued as a sponsor for years. After his funeral, the LCT came to my house and cooked for the service. I continued the relationship. We owned a hunting ranch in Crowell, Texas.

We donated use of our 10,000 square-foot lodge to the LCT's auctions during their yearly fundraiser. It was always a hit. I still volunteer as a team member. Alongside Ruthie the chef, I work in the kitchen on Mondays during the meetings.

The Ranch in Crowell used as a fundraiser.

I'm committed because I see the dedication of the team members who work events for twelve hours one day and show up bright and early the next morning when they're needed to work another. They're good people with great hearts. I like the fact that LCT is organized and has the facilities and equipment to do it right.

Dick Daugird Remembers Max Bowen

John Gannon and Max

I could write a book on Max. Over the years, he became one of my closest friends. He was a hard worker who started with nothing in life. As a young man early in his career Max climbed cell towers. He went on to eventually own his own cell tower company. His success allowed him to share his wealth with others less fortunate.

I remember seeing him at a FFA rodeo for kids in Santa Fe, Texas. He was feeling a little under the weather, but he still came out, bid on a calf, paid 5,000 dollars, and went home. I asked why he came out sick and he exclaimed, "To help the kids!"

He was a well-known figure at the Pasadena Livestock Show and Rodeo for his continued, unfailing support each year during various cook-offs and events.

Over 30 years ago, he invited me attend the Fort Lauderdale, Florida Boat Show because he knew I like boats.
I told him I'd have to pass on the trip.

Without a word, Max knew why. He was a bank director at my bank. He knew I didn't have the money to attend since I was raising a family and building a business.

Rather than embarrass me, he said, "Dick, I don't want to go alone. Would you oblige me and just keep me company? I'll pay your expenses and you'd be doing me a favor." We had a great time. It was the beginning of our long-term friendship and we remained good friends until he passed away.

Chapter Five

Veterans, Police, Clergy and the Mayor Tell Their Stories

Henry A. Trochesset
Sheriff
Galveston County

On behalf of Galveston County Sheriff's Office, I would like to recognize and give thanks to Lighthouse Charity Team for their dedication and commitment to our community. We appreciate their ongoing support of our citizens and improving the quality of life for others. They truly stand behind their motto, "People Helping People" and the positive impacts of their contributions are way too numerous to mention.

For over 30 years, this organization, led by Mr. Dick Daugird and wife, Mrs. Horacene Daugird, has helped feed thousands of people by providing food for events such as fundraisers and other non-profits, the less fortunate, medical patients and accident victims. They have also provided meals during disaster response and emergency assistance to man-made and natural disasters. This assistance proves invaluable to those going through stressful times and needing support. These efforts are all led by volunteers whose time and talent play a valuable role in our community.

Once again, our citizens are grateful that you have chosen Galveston County to call home.

Sincerely,

Henry Trochesset
Sheriff

To Protect and Serve
601 54TH STREET · SUITE 2100 · GALVESTON, TEXAS 77551 · PHONE: 409-766-2300

Chief Jeff Smith, Galveston Fire Department, Retired. Volunteer since 1986

Jeff loading water to take to Hurricane victims in Galveston.

I met Dick and Horacene in the mid 1980's. They were known within the Friendswood community for their great barbecue and could often be found cooking briskets, sausage and the like to support worthy causes. Those were the days before cell phones and email. Calls for volunteers were spread by word of mouth.

Prior to an event, two hundred briskets would be delivered to Dick's house. To prepare the meat for cooking required cutting it, rubbing it with seasoning and wrapping it.

Often Dick had no one to help. That's when a call would come into the Fire Station. Jeff said, "Dick, any chance you have a few people available to help out?" Firefighters are an easy group to rally; we do things in crews.

We immediately jumped into action, grabbed a radio and a called our fellow firefighters to help. Dick's barbecue was renowned and people were happy to help, especially because they were helping a charitable cause. Volunteers flocked in.

Over the years through my involvement with the LCT I've done everything I can to help. Their impact is felt throughout the community, especially during emergencies.

Hurricane Rita required all residents of Galveston Island to evacuate. Many lower income residents and seniors had no way off the island.

Buses were provided by the city and FEMA to help. Rita came roaring through the island and its impact was severe. Much of the island was flooded and many homes were lost. There was no power, fresh water or food.

A week after the storm passed through the island, the same people were bused back. The ten-hour ride home was grueling. Exhausted, confused and worried, they didn't know what they would face when they arrived home.

LCT sprang into action. They looked for every bottle of water they could find. Water was hard to come by then. Once more, Larry Del Papa sprang into action to help delivering two truck-loads of canned water.

Filling new plastic horse troughs donated by Tractor Supply with ice they hauled it to the bus depot. As each person got off the bus, they received a couple of bottles of water, a warm hug and a smile from the LCT volunteers. Instead of anger and confusion, there was immediate gratitude.

This gesture was so powerful it's become a standard part of the city's evacuation plan.

Joey "Blue Santa" Quiroga, Police Officer
Galveston 26 Years, Volunteer since 2015

Bicycles arrive and volunteers assemble. Gifts are wrapped in our meeting room by volunteers so officers can deliver toys before Christmas.

As a 26-year veteran of the Galveston Police Department, Joey Quiroga knows the importance of giving back. In addition to his

72

role as a full time police officer, Joey is an artist. He opened an art gallery in Galveston and one hundred percent of the proceeds go to the Blue Santa program providing Christmas gifts to needy children.

The LCT has supported Joey's cause since it began. They're on hand to help with the cooking at most Blue Santa fundraising events. The proceeds are used to buy Christmas toys for children in need. The LCT donates space in their 20,000 square foot Galveston location to store gifts. Then, over a weekend in December, "Santa's Elves" swoop in for two days, wrapping all the gifts. It's no small feat.

The Blue Santa Program started supporting 40 families and six years later is up to 2,000 families and still growing. The program was recently expanded to help children year round. "We might have a special needs child who needs an extra piece of equipment to help him get up, get around, walk, or make it to school," Joey said. "We're changing the direction somewhat."

Joey's Blue Santa program, combined with the LCT is a great example of *People Helping People*; in this case those people happen to be children.

Gordon Morse, retired Police Officer and volunteer since 2008

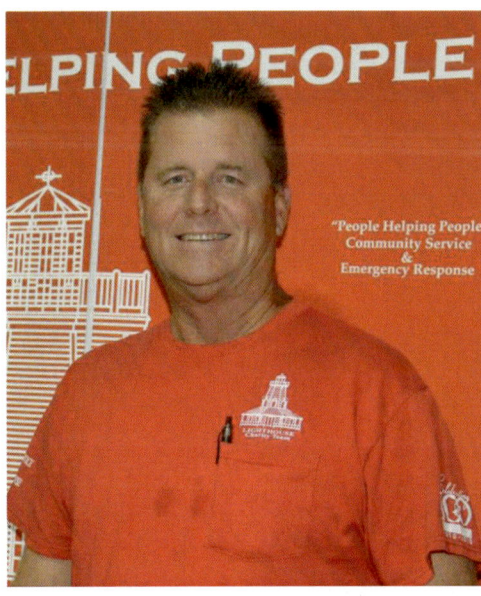

As a Galveston Police Officer I saw the LCT in the community on numerous occasions. After Hurricane Rita they were at Moody Methodist Church feeding displaced people from Louisiana. At the time, I didn't take much notice about the Team. I was too busy with my duties as a police officer; I just knew they handed out food.

Finally, in the aftermath of Hurricane Ike and during the island's recovery when food sources were scarce, I had the opportunity to eat several meals served by the LCT. I was surprised how delicious the food tasted. Typically, food served by disaster response organizations is simply "filler with little flavor." While I appreciate what these organizations do, they miss out on what a good, hot meal does for a human being going through a devastating experience. The food Lighthouse served was more than "filler," it was good. It takes you away from the trauma for a few minutes and sets you back at your mother's table where you felt cared for and safe. That did wonders for me and the other first responders lucky enough to discover this beacon of hope among the dreary surroundings after flooding, hurricanes and more.
I paid attention to the volunteers serving food. I noticed the care and concern they exhibited not just for the food and people they served, but also for each other. I took that memory with me and returned to work with higher spirits and greater hope for recovery.

Curious about this group of people, a few months after Hurricane Ike I looked up the LCT on the Internet to find out more. I sent an email to the founder, Dick Daugird thanking him for what he and the Lighthouse Charity Team do for the community and asked what I could do to help. Dick responded quickly, inviting me to his home.

I arrived to meet a man who is one of the most generous, caring people I've ever met. I made the decision right then and there to become part of the team.

I began volunteering and became part of the LCT family. We're kindred spirits with one mission - to help others. Honestly, it takes time, commitment, hard work and dedication for the volunteers to keep helping out. In the end, it's worth every drop of sweat, every ounce of effort, every hour given and every dollar spent.

There's no greater feeling, when at the end of an event you receive a heartfelt thank you and a warm hug. Ending the day with fellow team members, laughing and relaxing gives me a great feeling to know I've done something positive for others.

As individuals we can only do so much, but as a Team, nothing is impossible. It takes every single person, whether they donate their funds or their time. There are no titles. Every person is as important as the next, no matter what their status in life. It's what makes Lighthouse a true team.

My participation in Lighthouse is one of the best things I've ever done for myself. The people I've met, those we've helped, and the things we've done together as a team are experiences many will never know. As much as I'd like to say I've contributed to LCT, its actually the other way around. Lighthouse has given me more - family, friends and a powerful way to give back the blessings bestowed on me. Come join us.

Joe Giusti, Commissioner of Galveston County Volunteer and Sponsor since 2009

Joe and Dick, long time friends

I became a police officer for one reason; to help people. Getting involved in community service goes hand in hand. When I met the folks at the LCT, I realized they had the same attitude of service. Not only do they pitch in for the right reason, every penny that comes into the group goes back to the community.

My introduction to Lighthouse Charity Team was during Hurricane Ike in 2008. I'd recently retired from the Galveston Police Department as an officer and was working private security at the time.

I was volunteering on behalf of my company to help with clean up after Hurricane Ike. I met the LCT who served hot meals people working the clean-up. They were so genuine, real and happy. They seemed to care about the people they were serving. It made a positive impression on me.

A few months later I ran into Dick Daugird at an event and realized I was a client of his. My automobile and home insurance was with him for twenty-five years or more.

We talked about Lighthouse and he said, "Why don't you come join us?" So I did. I've volunteered for a lot of organizations over the years, and this one is absolutely the best group I've ever thrown my hat in the ring with.

During the wildfires in Bastrop and Smithville in 2011, I got an email from a Galveston police officer asking, "Hey, do you think we could borrow a barbecue pit?" Within 24 hours we had a private plane, forty volunteers, twenty trailers and trucks and 30,000 dollars of food and supplies on our way to feed the firefighters, police, military, and all the first responders dealing with the raging fires. We had no clue how long we'd be there. We just knew they needed us.

While we were In Bastrop, the ten year anniversary of 9/11 occurred. We ended up feeding the entire community that day as people gathered to remember 9/11. It was a special moment and we were proud to serve. I remember reading once that doing good for others makes you healthier and makes you feel good about yourself. I agree.

Dave and Susan Gillioz Volunteers since 2012 (former USMC)

Susan and I met Dick and his team while volunteering for Texas Equusearch in 2012. We were impressed with the level of professionalism and hard work every LCT Team member demonstrated.

As a Marine Corps veteran, I volunteer at events to raise money for veterans. One day we held an event to celebrate the 20th anniversary of our Vietnam Veterans of America (VVA) at Jack Brooks Park. More than 400 people showed up. The LCT was cooking. When it was time to pay for the food, I walked up to Dick and said, "Dick, you know how I am. I always like to square up at the end of every event. I'm ready for the bill."

Dick replied, "I think I'll just pick this bill up."

I said, "I'm not expecting you to."

He shot back, "Well, I'm doing it anyway." That opened my eyes to who Dick Daugird was, and I liked it.

The next weekend, LCT had a big event to raise money for a little nine-year-old girl fighting cancer. The event was held at a community pool. The day of the event, the weather was awful. It rained all day. We kept lifting the awning to let the water run off it. I felt sorry for the little girl and thought, "There is no way this event will raise any money for cancer." I was wrong. It was amazing. People showed up and we sold 1,207 dinners that day. It turned into a great event. Later I heard she conquered her cancer and went on to become a baton twirler in high school. Events like these for people in need keep Susan and I coming back. It's a great feeling to know you make a difference.

LCT not only helps others, but takes care of their volunteers as well. I went into the hospital this year with pneumonia and was there for five and a half days. About the third day here a huge basket of fruit arrived. In it was a card from the LCT that read, "Quit playing hooky and come back." I was missed.

I put in 129 hours last month and Susan volunteered 113 hours. We'll be here as long as the team needs us. They may be pushing us in a wheelchair, but we'll do something.

The best thing I can say about LCT is, "It's the slickest thing since pockets on shirts."

Mark Davis, Pastor, St. John's United Methodist Church, Baytown TX, Volunteer since 2005

Mark, at 6'6," who Dick affectionately calls "Shorty"

In 2005, as Co-founder and Executive Director of Gleaning from the Harvest, a local Galveston food pantry, I met Dick and other members of the LCT. We were honoring founder Bill Ritter and I was excited to see them cook at this event which provides food for Galveston's hungry.

I watched as the LCT pulled up with their shiny vehicle, trailer in tow. Our board and volunteers were prepared to help serve BBQ, chopped beef sandwiches, condiments, and chips. We fed over 150 people that day. Dick and Horacene were in the midst of it all, welcoming, serving and visiting with often-overlooked community members.

Dick, Horacene and the LCT are like family to me. They're always willing and able to assist whenever I ask. They've adopted me as "one of theirs." It's an honor to call them my family and brothers and sisters in Christ.

Chapter 6

Young Adults and Teens tell their Stories

Richard Daugird, Dick and Horacene's son and GM of Galveston LCT Operations

Growing up around the LCT taught me the value of helping others. As a kid I hung around the volunteers wanting to help. They kept me busy all the time, moving equipment, setting up chairs and tables and doing whatever needed to be done from start to finish of events.

At college, I studied drafting and engineering. I went to work in the Galveston area, but the economy went south. After losing a couple of jobs my Dad said, "Why don't you come work for me at the Lighthouse? We need your skills in design, maintaining the equipment."

So I did. At 23 years old, my dad saw me work with Larry of Acme Fabrication, designing the blueprints for "Grand Daddy," our biggest trailer. From that first trailer, along with the knowledge I gained in school, I've had a hand designing almost all our equipment.

Today I'm the General Manager over the LCT's Galveston Operation. I work with three other paid employees and we keep the building, vehicles and equipment in running order. Oftentimes we get equipment from our Friendswood Operation Center to repair. Yes, I get paid for working, however I volunteer a lot more of my time than I get paid for because I believe in the mission of *People Helping People*. Whether I'm volunteering for the Blue Santa program or designing a new trailer, I can't think of a better place to work. I hope to be contributing for many years to come.

Darla Winters, Dick and Horacene's daughter

I grew up surrounded by people cooking in our kitchen and on the barbecue pits in our backyard. Hardly a weekend went by when our home wasn't full of people. My parents were always at the center of the activity. When they weren't cooking, they were at festivals or parks serving food.

If my friends and I wondered what to do on a weekend, there were always opportunities to work with the team. I grew up within that environment of service and never gave much thought to the impact it made on our community.

Then came the Jerry Lewis Muscular Dystrophy (MDA) telethon. As a little girl I remember walking to the grocery store with the firemen and standing next to them as they collected money in their boots. The MDA event was the first time I finally understood the full impact of what we were doing.

Once I went away to college I was more removed from the LCT, but never removed from charitable service. It was part of my DNA. I joined the Food and Nutrition Club at college and helped cook meals for charitable causes. I was the spaghetti queen. Using the LCT recipe ensured our meals were always a big hit. After graduation I joined the Junior League and was drawn to the food booths where once again, my LCT cooking experience was valued. Today, I attend my kids' school carnivals and sporting events and am often in charge of the concession stands. It's what I know and where I can best serve. My kids now volunteer for Toys for Tots and Blue Santa. The Daugird family tradition of service is alive and well.

Robert Daugird, son of Dick and Horacene and volunteer

Robert with wife Tracy and son Matthew

Some people choose a charitable life but I was born into it. Like my sister Darla, we grew up surrounded by people working tire-lessly to give back. Being immersed in and surrounded by the service and giving back mentality provided me with a moral compass to know what it's like to help others. It shaped me into an individual who wanted to help.

I remember in elementary school spending time with the special needs kids who were often ignored by other kids. My upbringing taught me never to be afraid to help and to look at the situation, not the person. Therefore affliction didn't scare me or make me uncomfortable. I got my friends involved and we made great new friends with this special group of kids.

One of my favorite childhood memories happened when I was sixteen years old. A kid came to our house with his mom to talk with my mom about holding a fundraiser for her son. He had serious issues with his liver. While they talked, I looked over and saw him quietly sitting on the sofa. I invited him to play Nintendo and for the next hour we had a great time.

Ten years later I came home from college and he was onstage at an LCT event talking about how grateful he was for the help they gave him many years ago. Their assistance made it much easier on his family when he needed a liver transplant. His words were moving and every team member present had a smile on their face as they listened.

I met my wife at Texas A&M. I brought her home to meet my parents and we found them working at an event. As I introduced her I said, "Here's my parents and fifty other people who are like my family." We've been married twenty-two years and each time we come home we see a lot of the same "family" we've seen for years. The LCT environment is one of inclusion. It's a wide variety of people who are all like family.

Today I'm involved with the Catholic organization, The Knights of Columbus. I often work in the kitchen frying fish. I bring my fifteen-year-old son Matthew and he's willing to do anything; take out the trash, washing up, etc. I want him to understand being involved helping others instills a mission of fulfillment, a sense of doing something bigger than each one of us. His grandparents have understood this for years.

My experiences with LCT also taught me important management lessons. I learned when you have a group of volunteers you need to delegate a role to each person, like handling a food station, overseeing the beverage trailer or helping people park cars. Delegating roles gives people a sense of purpose and ownership. I use that strategy with my business team today. Like my parents know, when you make people "owners" of your business, you can do a lot with just a few.

As I look to the future, my hope for the LCT is they continue serving the community for another 30 years.

Scott Gordon volunteer since 1990 and future leader of LCT

I was at home one evening in June of 1990 when the phone rang. I answered it and it was my friend Robert Daugird, Dick's son. "Scott," he said, "What are you doing in the morning?"

"Not much," I replied, "Why?"

"Well, my Dad has a charity called the LCT. We're holding an event tomorrow morning to welcome home the troops from the Gulf War and we need help. A local businessman bought the reserve grand champion steer at the Houston Livestock Show and Rodeo and he asked us to do something good with it, so we are."

"Sure," I said, without thinking. "I'll be there. What time do you need me?"

"Great," he replied. "Meet us at 5:30 a.m."

I showed up and Robert introduced me to his father Dick who said, "Nice to meet you. Now get a shirt and put on an apron, then do whatever people tell you to do."

Dick, as a young man and Scott when he was a teenager.

I wasn't sure I belonged here but followed orders and worked doing whatever was needed until 9:30 that morning when the ice truck showed up. Dick yelled, "Robert! Get your buddy there and go unload the ice truck."

We opened the back of the truck and there was five thousand pounds of ice in ten pound bags. For hours we unloaded ice while I thought "this isn't where I want to be". As the day continued I watched everyone, including Dick, work hard. At the end of the event Robert and I loaded up equipment and drove it back to the FOC. As we were unloading, Dick walked up to me, slapped me on the back, shook my hand, thanked me, and said, "What are you doing tomorrow morning?"

I showed up Sunday morning and began my lifetime of helping others.

The Gordon Family-Citizens of the Year Friendswood, Texas

Heather Gordon: Wife of Scott and volunteer for 19 years

It all started with a blind date. Scott and I hit it off from the moment we met. As he talked about the LCT, I asked a simple question, "Anything I can do to help?" He immediately invited me to attend an event the next morning. I showed up, was told to put on an apron and escorted to the serving line. That's how I started my journey helping this great group.

Dick and Horacene are an important part of our family. Dick has played multiple roles in Scott's life – dad, boss and friend. He and Horacene treat Scott like a son and he considers them adopted parents. In fact, when Scott and I got married, Dick was his best man. With the dedication they have to the LCT, it was inevitable that I would, too. I loved it. The serving line became my specialty and I enjoyed working with the team and meeting new people at every event.

When our son Cole was born, my role with the Team changed to behind the scenes support. With a full time job and a baby, I still found time to help.

One of my favorite memories of Scott and Cole was coming home from work one day and seeing a sight that makes me smile when I remember. Scott had baby Cole, on the golf cart, strapped into his walker with an umbrella over his head. They were pulling out of the driveway as I was pulling in, headed to an event being held at the LCT building next door. Both had giant grins on their faces.

When Cole was younger, nothing worked better as a disciplinary tool than banning him from working with the team and making him watch an event from the inside our house. Cole is committed to the LCT. As a mom, I try to keep a balance between his schoolwork and helping at charity events.

Married almost 19 years now, though at times we've had to juggle schedules, miss important events and work around the clock to prepare, I wouldn't trade our involvement with the LCT for anything. It's been part of my life since the moment I first put on that apron.

The hard work and commitment of time can be overwhelming. However, when you see the end result, helping another family or organization, it's truly gratifying. I'm committed to helping Scott ensure the LCT remains strong for many years to come.

Cole Gordon, son of Scott and Heather, now age 15

Cole started young - he was born into the Team

I'll do whatever is needed, no matter what. I've basically done about anything you can do on this team except drive trailers and I'm looking forward to the day I get my driver's license. I love working with the Team. Our volunteers are busy, but they make the time to work and have fun while doing it. I learned from my dad and mom how important it is to help others, and it's what I enjoy. After school, weekends, summers, and outside of school, it's become my life.

I remember the first event I was in charge of and the pride I felt when everything went well. I was 10 years old and we were at McRee Ford in Dickinson raising funds for the food bank and church. We served over one thousand people that day. It was my first Gray Hat Team leader role and I was proud.

I've had people suggest, "Let's start a junior lighthouse for kids." I tell them it would be hard to find kids who want to work that hard. They'd love the free food, but not necessarily the work. It's tough, and until you understand why you're doing it, you won't enjoy it like I do.

I've found ways to take the LCT's work to my school. This weekend we're cooking during Friendswood High School's Football game. Members of the Marching Band will join our volunteers and the funds will go to help their Booster Club. As the manager of the varsity football team, I'm proud to be able to bring my school and the LCT together for a good cause.

Chapter 7

The Third Ingredient - Sponsors

While volunteers are critical to charity organizations, sponsors are the lifeblood. They primarily keep the organization afloat through their financial support. When they believe in a cause, they'll write the check, donate equipment or support the annual fundraiser with donated items for the live auction. The secret to obtaining and maintaining long-term sponsorships is to develop friendships. Sponsors, like volunteers, have many choices. To make your charity their choice, don't make the relationship one-sided. If you want to attract a good sponsor, be one. This may sound contradictory, after all, aren't you looking for sponsors, not looking to give things away?

Yes, but, as Theodore Roosevelt said, "No one cares how much you know, until they know how much you care." As a cooking organization, you can approach potential sponsors with the offer of cooking for their major events. It's a win/win. They'll save money on the cost of their event, and you'll build a valuable relationship. It may take a few attempts, but it works. Once again, Lorraine Grubbs shares her wisdom and experience from the business world and how it applies to the non-profit arena.

For example, I recently attended an event at Larry Del Papa's headquarters. The event was a celebration Larry was having for the local distributors of their products. The LCT was present, cooking and serving food. Not only did they get to visit with each person coming through the food line, Dick, Horacene and Scott were on hand to network.

The LCT was only too happy to help Larry, one of their most loyal sponsors with this event. In this way Dick, Horacene and everyone who's part of the LCT were able to repay him or at least show their appreciation, in a small way for the many times he's been there for them.

Cash is king, but in-kind trade works well too. LCT cooks for the employees of Southwest Airlines during their yearly Houston employee celebration. Instead of paying cash, Southwest Airlines trades airline tickets and LCT uses them for future fundraisers, a true win/win.

Scott Gordon has taken the lead in this area of the Team. He takes the time to visit various sponsors to help when needed. They've developed deep relationships with their sponsors and as a result sponsors are always in the background willing to help with money, equipment, and in-kind donations, many times donating without even being asked.

According to Dick Daugird, "Most donor names don't appear on any of the trailers or equipment because the true meaning of helping people is to not try to score anything in return. If a donor provides a truck or trailer at no cost and their desire is to have their name on the trailer this is a consideration we occasionally approve."

Our sponsors donate as little as 100 dollars to over 100,000 dollars annually. Some give of their time, others give money. Our organization depends on sponsors to do what we do. Donations are received in various denominations of cash, check, credit card, and PayPal. One man even offered us gold teeth.

LCT sponsors are every bit as loyal as the volunteers and we're so grateful for their support. We wouldn't be the organization we are today without them. Selfless, dedicated and generous, we appreciate each and every one."

Sponsor Testimonials

John Gannon and his wife Lettie, Sponsors for over 20 years

John owns JGI Outdoor Advertising Company in Katy, Texas serving the Texas and Louisiana area by providing large billboards.

Dick recalls: I met John about twenty years ago after a church service at Mary Queen Catholic Church in Friendswood. The LCT was cooking for the Church Festival. John came over during the event and introduced himself, asking, "How are you doing?" "Not too well," I responded. "One of our refrigerators just went out on the trailer."

John immediately offered to drive me to his ranch in Gonzales Texas to pick up a refrigerated trailer he donated. It was like a dream come true. We still use "Cool Daddy" today. After some reworking it's still just as good as new.

Good friend John Gannon and his wife Lettie, Sponsors for over 20 years

As our friendship grew, we found we had a lot in common. One thing is we share the same birthday though he's a bit younger. Neither of us had a formal college education. We both started our own businesses at a young age without much capital. We both learned the importance of giving back. The LCT is only one of many organizations John supports with his charitable giving. John's been a faithful supporter of our annual January fundraiser and is one of the first to make an advance reservations for not one but two tables. Then he invites his employees and friends to enjoy the event.

In addition to the fundraiser support, over the years John has donated the use of his billboard space at no charge to LCT and other charities with whom we've requested his help. I'm grateful for my friend John's help. He's definitely a man who lives our motto, *People Helping People*.

Rex Baggett, Owner, Copy Doctor. Sponsor since 2007

I met Scott Gordon and Heather through my children. Both of our kids attended the same elementary school. During the annual fundraising carnival for the school, Scott and the LCT were present, cooking and serving.

We continued running into each other at many different events in our community and neighborhood over the next two years. I thought, "Wow, what nice people. They seem to volunteer a lot." I had no idea the extent to which they were involved in charity work.

One day Scott called and asked if I could print some raffle tickets for a fundraiser being held for a sick child. I immediately agreed and told him I'd deliver the tickets. The next day, with tickets in hand I pulled into the LCT's location and asked for Scott. "He's in the back shed," someone told me.

I walked into the shed and stopped in my tracks. The "shed" was huge. I looked around and saw trailers, trucks and lots of cooking equipment. As Scott approached I said, "Are you kidding me? I thought you had a food truck. I've known you two years and you never described the magnitude of this operation. This is amazing! If I didn't know how big your operation is, then others probably don't, either. You need a brochure to hand out at your events to let people know what you do."

That's how my mission to spread the word about the LCT started. I became a self-appointed marketing guy and put together their first brochure. I wanted to tell their story so when they sought sponsors they wouldn't be seen as just a cooking team, rather as a powerful contributor to the community and other charities. I wanted to show their effect on first responders in emergency situations.

Other than the military, I knew of no other group serving first responders. More importantly in all their efforts, they were using their own funds. Their operation was a finely tuned machine and could be deployed within a couple of hours notice.

Their volunteers are the salt of the earth and just want to help out. Over the years I've helped them with newsletters, handouts and just about any printed product they needed. I'm proud I can help this fine group of folks who want no credit, no glory for what they do.

If I can contribute my services and spread the word about the good they do, then I've done my part.

Todd Nelms: JMH Blast Coat, Sponsor since 2003

I initially supported the LCT because they were in my neighborhood. It gave me a chance to keep my donations local and see the effect firsthand.

My wife Kim and I began volunteering with the LCT spending time in the kitchen, cooking for events. One day a refrigerator trailer called *Cool Daddy*, (donated by John Gannon) had a mishap and flipped over on its side. I took it to my shop and repaired it.

That was the start of my mission to repair, repaint and refurbish the cooking trailers. Slowly all the equipment took on the same color theme: silver, black and red.

Our next project involved buying a used twenty-foot long car hauler and turning it into "Grand Baby,*"* complete with rotisserie, serving line, refrigeration, braising pan and a full sink. It was capable of serving up to three hundred fifty people per hour.

The projects kept coming. Next, I took *Beverage Daddy*, stripped it down, gutted it and rebuilt the interior of the trailer with a new ice maker, air ride suspension, and gave it a fresh, new coat of paint. *Toddler*, and *Grand Daddy* followed in line with retrofits.

We had a Kenworth motorhome in the fleet, donated by Dick and Horacene. It was used to give team members a place to take breaks during events. We upgraded it as well.

Over the years as Kim and I look back, some of our most profound moments are when we helped sick children through tough times. To see those kids later as young adults in the community gave us a great feeling of satisfaction. All in all, the LCT is a well thought out organization that does a lot of good for people going through difficult times.

Boyd Yarbrough President: Elite Surgical Affiliates, Sponsor since 2010

I met the LCT at their annual fundraising gala six years ago. Meeting Dick, Scott and Horacene, I immediately saw their vision and their passion. As I heard about their involvement with first responders and the effort to which they went to care for people in need, it spoke to me.

After meeting their Team Members, I realized these were people who provided resources, with smiling faces, to those in need during troubled times.

My wife Leslie and I are grateful to be in a position to give back. While we also support valuable organizations like Project Healing Waters, The Folds of Honor and St Jude, upon meeting the LCT, we realized this was an organization where we could see the impact our donations were having firsthand. Convinced this was a highly worthwhile cause, we became enthusiastic sponsors.

We may not be on the front lines cooking and serving, but we've definitely contributed to the funding that keeps the team going. One of our favorite events is the Blue Santa Program held every Christmas in Galveston. Our kids Max and Malorie get involved in helping collect, wrap and deliver toys for kids who would otherwise get nothing during the holidays. We hope by participating our kids see how fortunate they are.

Our involvement with the LCT has positively impacted my family. Our daily goal is to wake up each morning and make a difference. Whether giving someone a kind word or helping those in need, we're fulfilling our values by supporting an organization like the LCT. These folks make a difference in the lives of first responders and victims of tragedies and natural disasters.

Volunteering teaches character and humility while creating opportunities to do God's work.

Mitchell Dale, VP and General Manager McCree Ford, Sponsor Since 1986

We've had the pleasure of being affiliated with the LCT for thirty years. I met Dick many years ago when he bought a truck from us. As the General Manager of my family's business, I went out to personally thank him. We shook hands and he said, "Treat me right, and you'll have a customer for life!" That was great to hear until I realized he only bought a new car every 15 years.

One of our core values at McCree Ford is making a difference in the communities we serve. When I realized what Dick and his team did, it was a perfect fit for us. Over the years we've provided them with all the Ford trucks in their fleet. The LCT has helped us with a number of our fundraisers such as Drive 4 UR Community.

We've stuck with the LCT because they have a strong commitment to serve people in our community. They do so with a smile and an attitude of service. They're consistent in their actions and never deviate from their mission of *People Helping People*.

Mr. and Mrs. William "Bill" Dale, founders of McRee Ford

I'm most impressed with their volunteers. They're fun, committed and possess a servant's heart. The energy in their organization is contagious and consistent.

Dick is an impressive leader. It would be easy to write a check, give orders and send people off, but he and Horacene are physically present at the majority of their events. He may be sitting down if he's under the weather, but the smile on his face as he shakes your hand and greets you is genuine. A leader who walks their talk is much more credible.

I also believe in being at our events. You get a different feeling seeing the camaraderie, smiles and gratitude on people's faces. One event we participated in with the LCT made a huge impression on me. The event was held to raise funds to help a critically ill little girl in Dickinson. The morning of the event it poured. We anticipated no one would be there, yet hundreds showed up and we sold out of food by noon. The look on the faces of her family was priceless.

Vision, commitment, and dedication. The LCT has demonstrated, over the years they're consistent in these principles. It's never about them, always about others. Regardless of the obstacles in their path, they stick to their mission through thick and thin. I like to think of them as missionaries in our area. I'm grateful to have them as part of our family.

Joe Stanfield, sponsor since 2010

My childhood friend Bill came down for the weekend to stay on my boat in Clear Lake, Texas. Hurricane Ike ripped up the area a couple of months earlier and the community was rebuilding damaged homes, businesses, marinas, etc.

The Beach Boys were playing a benefit concert at Moody Gardens in Galveston to benefit the hurricane relief organizations. I thought it would be fun to take the boat from my home slip in Kemah to Offatts Bayou in Galveston to see the concert.

We loaded up the boat with food and libations and made our way to the anchorage at Offatts (a three hour boat ride). We got there about noon and picked a great spot to anchor not far from the stage.

We lowered the dinghy into the water, had lunch and congratulated ourselves for positioning our boat in a premiere spot to watch the evening concert. Not so fast... as we settled down, ready to enjoy the leisurely afternoon, we discovered we had NO BEER. I mean NO BEER! How can you possibly take it easy and enjoy an afternoon on your boat without BEER?

I remembered seeing a convenience store further up the Bayou. Since I had a couple of things to do on the boat, I talked my friends Bill and Dawna into taking the dinghy to search for BEER, explaining where the store was located. When they left, I went about doing my chores on the boat and awaited their return.

An hour later, they returned with a case of Budweiser® Beer. I was happy. As we put it in the ice chest and settled down for a cold one they said, "Hey, Joe, we've got something to tell you." I listened patiently as they told me how they went up the Bayou toward the store and found a dock to tie up the dinghy. As they got out of the boat and stepped onto the dock a big, tall guy came out and said, "Hey you can't tie up here, it's a private dock." Then he asked them what they were doing. They told him they were going to buy beer. That immediately put the big guy in a better mood. He had the same affection for beer as we did.

He introduced himself as Dick and noticed their dinghy named "Small Change". Dick drove around the bayou earlier and noticed "Daddy's Money" at anchor by Moody Gardens. He asked them if they were on that boat.

They replied, "Yes."

Happily Dick told them he had a group of people coming out on their party barge for the concert and would tie up to us. "We can all party together," Dick said. He pulled out a case of Bud and gave it to them. He wouldn't take any money and just said, "It's all about *People Helping People*."

My whole afternoon was ruined. All I could think about was a barge load of big rednecks coming out, wanting to tie up to my boat. I'd never let any boat tie up to Daddy's Money. The craft is immaculate. There are no scuff marks on the deck, no dings on the side of the boat from docks or other boats.

I imagined big rednecks with cowboy boots pirating my boat, spilling sticky drinks all over my pristine deck. My afternoon was ruined and I fretted away what was left of the day.

As the sun set, sure enough, along came Dick around the bend with a barge full of people in the bayou heading right toward Daddy's Money. I immediately got out all the fenders I had to make sure the barge didn't bump into my perfectly white fiber-glass hull. I thought the steel barge could do a lot of damage to my boat especially if this guy can't drive.

The moment arrived and he pulled alongside handling the barge like a pro. He gently maneuvered it into place, threw us lines and secured the barge alongside. I walked over and this big tall guy stuck out his hand for a shake. With that big smile and friendly voice we began conversing, drinking and listening to the Beach Boys.

The night flew by quickly as our friendship developed my fear of a barge full of big rednecks diminished. I learned about the charity Dick and Horacene started and became acquainted with some Team members. At the end of the night they invited us to bring Daddy's Money to their dock and tie up the next morning for brunch.

This started my great friendship with not only Dick and Horacene but also with the Lighthouse Charity Team and its Team Members. It all happened over one case of Budweiser® Beer, and *People helping People.*

The Honorable David J.H. Smith, Former Mayor of Friendswood

The LCT consistently responds to those in need, and our community is better for it. They bring a sense of stability and security knowing they always can be found in times of need. Helping others comes naturally to the volunteers who work with the LCT.

They see the results of their efforts in the faces of those they serve. It's a reward only a true servant of man can appreciate. As part of our community family, just knowing the LCT is here, ready and willing, gives us a great sense of confidence.

Chapter 8

Ready? Checklist for the Rest of the Ingredients

You've heard the story of Lighthouse Charity Team and the stories of some of the people who make it work. Now we'd like to present you with a blueprint, based upon ours. ANY community or organization can use it to build their own cooking charity team. Here you'll find the nine vital steps to make it happen.

You might be surprised to discover the first objective we recommend isn't about gathering a crew of volunteers, instead it's about determining the "people values" your organization will live by, year in and year out.

This chapter will also guide you through the nitty-gritty process of choosing a name, a logo, a slogan and your social media presence. You'll also be introduced to the ins and outs of setting up a 501C (3) or non-profit status for the Internal Revenue Service. Toward the end of the chapter, you'll read a touching story about a little boy LCT helped out many years ago that brings everything together.

Step 1: Establish Your Basic "People" Values

This important step is the foundation of your organization. It's the measuring stick by which you live. Everything you do and anyone who volunteers with and sponsors the organization should align with your principles and values. Here are examples of values that'll serve you well:

- Lead with Honesty
- Have Character
- Exhibit Integrity
- Possess Faith
- Demonstrate Love
- Let go of ego
- Capacity for loyalty

These values are at the heart of LCT and could be your basic values, too. They should be non-negotiable when "hiring volunteers" and accepting sponsors and event partners. Other important points to remember:

Maintain a frugal mindset. This will allow you to grow without the burden of liabilities and long-term debt.

Lead by example. Walk the Talk. Do what you say you'll do.

Step 2: Name, Logo, Slogan and Website

This is the second step in setting up your foundation. Once your values and principles are identified, you need a good name appropriate to what you do. You also need a slogan to reflect who you are. Remember the LCT story of starting out as a "Cooking Team" then changing the name to a "Charity Team" to better reflect what they do. Once your name is established, you'll want to spread the word about your organization. The easiest way to do it in today's world is through social media.

- Pick a name for your non-profit. If you're unsure about a name, ask potential sponsors, volunteers and members of the community to help. In this way you might avoid the experience LCT had when they changed their name midstream. *Low Cost Tip: Invite potential volunteers and sponsors to lunch and explain what you're doing. Ask for help coming up with a name. This way they're involved from the start.*

- Once you have a name, create a logo and slogan. They'll be important communicating your brand. LCT picked a lighthouse. The slogan is "People Helping People."   Take some time making these decision. It's how people will identify with you and how your volunteers will represent you. It need not cost a lot. *Low Cost Tip: Go to fiverr.com or upwork.com. These sites are where you can find freelancers including graphic artists to inexpensively bid on your job.*

- Obtain a permanent mailing address. It can be separate from your building location. A post office box works fine.

- Get a phone number. LCT uses a permanent landline that forwards all calls to their cell phone, 24 hours a day, seven days a week.

- Print business cards once you have your name and logo. *Low Cost Tip: Contact a local printer and see if there's an opportunity to help with an event they have coming up in exchange for this and future printing needs.*

- Establish a website. Don't worry about being "fancy." A one-page "landing page" format will serve you well. *Low Cost Tip: Check with your local Chamber of Commerce for names or read a book like "Websites for Dummies."*

- Set up a Facebook, Twitter and Instagram Account. *Low Cost Tip: Almost any teenager today can help you.*

Step 3: Set up a 501 (C) 3

Now that you have your name, slogan and logo, it's time to obtain a 501 (C) 3 designation. This is where you'll wisely spend early capital. Hiring a good attorney and CPA will keep you on the right path from the onset.

- Locate an Attorney and CPA to set up a corporation and a 501 (C) 3. *Low Cost Tip: Ask an attorney you have a good relationship with to help you with the costs. Sometimes they'll donate their time working for you pro bono. Similar to the case with the printer, offer to help cook for a favorite charity event in exchange for legal fees.*

- Get a good CPA who understands non-profits. Establish the minimum level of donation your donors can take a tax deduction on. LCT's is $250. Check with your CPA for a more detailed description.

- Be aware of IRS rules regarding perks for volunteers, politicians, etc. For example, IRS guidelines prohibit putting a politician's bumper sticker on any equipment or supporting/promoting him or her in many other ways.

Step 4: You have the basics down, now what?

These next steps may seem basic, but we include them because they indeed are an important part of the process of setting up your own charity.

- Dick and Horacene had a talent for cooking barbecue. Can you cook? If not, learn how or find someone who can.

- Beg, borrow or build your first barbecue pit on a trailer with the help of volunteers to get them interested in being part of your group or team.

- To start finding volunteers and sponsors, offer to use the barbecue pit to cook for a community event, sports team, Scouts, school or Church fundraiser using your volunteer labor.

Step 5: Recipe for Finding Volunteers

Why is volunteering important to people? It's vital to understand the basic nature of volunteers. It's a common mistake to think volunteering is just something nice people can do. Yes, it may make them feel great about helping, but what impact does it really have? Volunteers have an enormously positive impact on the health and wellbeing of our communities.

Our cities, suburbs, towns and all the wide spaces in-between wouldn't be what they are without the generosity of volunteers. Volunteers deliver critical services from serving as neighborhood fire fighters, participating in search and rescue missions, delivering meals to homebound seniors, patrolling the neighborhood to keep it safe, tutoring and mentoring young people and much more. They're the lifeblood of a community and they'll be the lifeblood of your organization.

As mentioned earlier, communicate the essential value of volunteers' time to them. Look at statistics like hours served and the economic dollar value of volunteered time. LCT tracks all the volunteer hours. The sizable sum it grows into is amazing. Their volunteers share that value with all the Team Members. It allows them to show their deep appreciation and thank their volunteers.

Tips for finding volunteers

- Try to recruit a few members from the event you're working. Many times people willing to jump in and help will have an interest in becoming a regular volunteer.

- If you already have volunteers ask them for referrals. Existing volunteers are great sources for referrals to new volunteers.

- Retirees make great volunteers. They're usually looking for something meaningful to do, they enjoy helping others, they bring skills from past occupations, and they enjoy the camaraderie belonging to a team environment brings.

- Get families involved in volunteering. Husband and wife teams often make great volunteers.

- Older kids can be a good source. By volunteering, they learn the value of giving back. Make sure they're over 12 years old so they understand any safety issues that might be involved.

- Single people also make great volunteers. This gives them a chance to meet others. Who knows, they might meet the love of their life helping out as a volunteer.

- If you hold a focus group to help you select a name as mentioned earlier, don't forget to ask for their help in obtaining volunteers.

- Set up guidelines for your volunteers regarding their appearance, food handling protocol, alcohol consumption and other rules.

Imagine if one day no one showed up anywhere in your community to volunteer. What would happen? What would our cities, towns, schools, churches, and libraries across America look like? What basic needs would people go without?

You probably cross paths with a volunteer at least once if not more every day. Take the time to thank them. From the start, show your appreciation to those who help your organization. Appreciation is a great tool for creating loyalty.
One of Dick's favorite saying is, "A stranger is a friend we have not met yet." Recruit your volunteers with that mindset and you'll stand a far greater chance of successfully attracting and retaining the right volunteers.

Step 6: Hold Regular Meetings

Establishing a regular meeting time and place is fundamental to good communication. Volunteers, like employees, need to be on the same page as the organization and regular meetings inform and organize the team.

- Start having regular meetings at someone's house, garage, local chamber office, Church hall or other meeting room in the community.

- Establish regular times and stick to them. LCT has a meeting each Monday at their Galveston location and on Tuesdays in the Friendswood location. The only exception to this is if the day falls on a holiday.

- Each location has a similar format for meetings:
  o Board meetings are held from 4:00 -5:00 p.m.,
  o Social hour is from 5:00 - 6:00 p.m., and
  o The all-volunteer group meeting from 6:00-6:45 p.m.

- Board meetings include board members and are open to all team members to discuss event requests and other business not conducive to a large group. Be respectful of your volunteers' time and keep meetings on track.

- Team Meetings include dinner for a voluntary five dollar charge. Volunteers usually prepare it, but could also be food purchased locally, like pizza etc.

- Encourage new members to tell the group about themselves and bring in an occasional guest speaker. LCT usually has twenty five to fifty volunteers show up at each meeting. Keep the size of your meeting room in mind and plan accordingly.

- Get guest speakers from past events or upcoming events. You're limited when it comes to allowing politicians to campaign at your location. See IRS guidelines.

- Record minutes at all meetings

Step 7: Equipment and Building Needs

As you set up the logistics of your new charity, make sure you establish a headquarters location. Garages, church basements, and community centers are good starter buildings, especially when first starting out. It need not be fancy, just functional.

Dick remembers where his organization got started. "LCT first started by pouring a fifteen by twenty foot concrete slab at our residence. It was used to park the cooking trailer on week-ends for various events. When not in use the trailer was stored at a storage facility. We now have 38,700 square feet of enclosed building space."

- Find a location to work from and store your trailer and equipment out of the weather. Consider using your garage, a vacant building that might be donated or loaned to your organization or a local business that'll allow you to store your equipment free of rent until you find something more permanent.

- Minimum equipment needed: Sinks, refrigeration, flat top grill, and stove. This could be mounted on a trailer until your organization grows in size and is able to move into a commercial kitchen.

- As part of your branding, create a color scheme for your equipment so it all blends together. The LCT's trucks, trailers, clothing etc. are all red.

- Have aprons, hats and shirts either screen printed or embroidered so your volunteers are all dressed alike. Use the same color scheme as your equipment. *Low Cost Idea: Include your sponsor names on these items to become partners.*

Step 8: Finding Good Food Sources

Because you are a "cooking" charity, like a restaurant, you need to establish where you'll buy your food. Besides equipment, food will be one of your biggest costs. By streamlining where you buy it, you'll help keep costs low.

- Find a local wholesale grocer to deliver food. LCT started purchasing food at Sam's Club and eventually got big enough to have food was delivered to their site.

- Eventually, as you grow, you'll need a pallet jack or forklift to unload pallets.

Step 9: Sponsors - Where to find them, how to get them

As stated earlier, sponsors, like volunteers, are the lifeblood of your charity. Organizations just starting out often dread asking for money. But if your mission is solid, your communication stellar and your leaders dedicated, it'll be easier to find similar-minded individuals who want to help you. Here are some tips.

- Don't be afraid to ask for help. Look among your own friends, neighbors and business associates, basically the people who already know, like and respect you. They'll want to support you and it'll build your confidence to start going after other sponsors. *Low Cost Tip: Don't forget to ask them for a minimum of three referral sponsors.*

- Attend local meetings with your Chambers of Commerce, Rotary and Lions Clubs and other service organizations. Tell your story and share your mission by being a guest speaker.

- Research those companies who give donations to charitable organizations. Prepare a grand request as another source of funding. *Low Cost Tip: Go to companies' websites and see if and who they support with donations, then contact them about your organization.*

When working with sponsors, make sure you establish a policy your organization's name is the only one that'll go on a trailer. This ground rule encourages the types of sponsors who truly want to help versus one who only wants to use your organization for advertising their business.

There will be times you'll want to advertise for sponsors. Make sure you have a policy about what level of donation receives what amount of exposure. Naturally, a $100 sponsor will receive less recognition than a $10,000 sponsor.

Above all, develop friendships with your sponsors. *Low Cost Tip: Discover facts about them worth remembering like their birthday, family names, pet names, favorite candy, food or restaurant, etc. Then, as a first step, send them a card on their birthday with a sample of their favorite candy or a small gift card for their favorite restaurant. You'll be stunned how far this small cost-effective effort will go.*

Chapter 9

Events: Size, Logistics, Planning and Executing

LCT is a first responder in emergency situations like fires, floods, tornadoes and hurricanes. For example, when Hurricane IKE hit Houston and Galveston in 2008, their volunteers, along with those from first United Moody Methodist Church, provided meals for more than 50,000 affected people.

Whether it's a man-made or natural disaster, LCT is well equipped to handle humanitarian relief throughout Galveston County. When adequate food is available, LCT is prepared to sustain emergency responders and residents of affected areas for long periods of time.

They provide hot, cooked meals including an entrée, vegetable, starch, roll, salad, dessert and water. They can vary their menus for longer-term assignments. So, it's important to understand the logistics for each event including:

- How many people
- Where it will be held
- How many volunteers are needed and
- What equipment is necessary?

This is an important part of managing all aspects of your business or charity.

Event Planning

From the beginning, establish processes for handling your events. Think through and discuss how to handle with each detail of the event from the first call to food ordering, prep, volunteer assignments, on-site management, clean up and debriefing. By addressing and planning for these issues ahead of time, it will help organize your team and avoid miscommunication. LCT suggests these guidelines for event planning:

- Having three to six weeks advance notice prior to a planned event will give you adequate time for planning.

When you start out, however, you may not get that much notice. Make sure your volunteers understand "at the drop of a hat" emergency service.

- Pick one volunteer to head up an event. Choose a person responsible enough to take the lead on everything from start to finish.

- Being chosen should be an honor, not a chore.

- The system at LCT is called the "The Gray Hat" method. Whoever's chosen to lead an event selects a colored hat. All volunteers wear that same colored hat at the event so they're easily recognizable.

- Always have "Plan B" ready in case of bad weather. Rain dates or an alternate inside hall or venue should be discussed with the partner organization.

- Drive-through events are popular with busy people. Make it easy for hungry people to drive through your location and pick up their meals on their way home.

- Sell tickets ahead of time so you know how much food to prepare.

- Food raffles, live and silent auctions make the most money.

- Create a checklist for each event with all equipment and food needed.

- Decide how you'll get paid for the food you purchase for the event. Set up credit with the organization you're working with and settle up at the end of the event. There's no charge for LCT's volunteer labor and use of equipment because they consider this as their share of the donation.

- They charge for the actual cost of food, propane, wood and other supplies.

- Have event planners sell advance tickets. Food waste results in lost profits. This will give you a better idea of how many meals to prepare.

What should you do with leftover food? Agree ahead of the event what to do with it such as donating to a local charity, Food Bank, The Salvation Army, etc. Another way to utilize leftovers is by coordinating with your partner organization to continue the sale of meals at a different or better location, furthering their fundraising efforts.

Dick recalls a story about leftover food

One time a local Rotary Club decided to sell pork ribs at an event. They must've let their stomach do the planning as we had over one hundred uncut slabs of ribs left over. They asked us what to do. Obviously, the leftover ribs had to be donated or sold the next day, which happened to be a Sunday. We put on our thinking caps and came up with a plan. The next morning we went to a busy lake, set up our trailer at the boat ramp and sold the leftover cooked slabs of ribs to boaters headed out for the open water. We sold out and they thought we were geniuses!

The moral of the story is always devise a "legal escape route" to get the most money for the charity you're helping by marketing any remaining fresh food, cooked or uncooked, to other folks. Keep current on your health code certificates so you have the opportunity to sell leftover food at different opportunities like the example above.

Activating Your Volunteer Team

You are ready to activate your team. You've prepared, discussed, organized and planned. There are two primary types of events you'll deal with: scheduled events and last-minute emergencies. Below are suggestions from the LCT on how to handle both types of events.

Scheduled Events: When a call is placed to the LCT by a person or organization who wants to put on an event, they're asked questions to determine the individual or organization's eligibility for their services.

1. Upon meeting the required criteria the LCT Board get together to make sure the event fits our schedule and our capabilities.

2. LCT then meets with the event coordinators for the non-profit to further determine details like the date, location, theme, menu, etc.

3. LCT commits to doing the organization's event, providing the food.

4. Events are usually planned up to six weeks in advance to allow for promotional advertising etc. During this time LCT provides coaching to the event planners so they know what to expect.

5. A confirmed headcount the week of the event is necessary to estimate food needs. LCT orders food from Gordon Food Service, who gives them a wholesale price.

6. At the event their volunteers cook the food on site with their large mobile cooking trailers. They make sure they meet all health codes.

7. LCT requests the benefitting organization handle all monies collected. The organization then pays the food bill and any associated expenses.

Unscheduled Events: These are events that occur suddenly such as an accident, a natural or man-made disasters. With emergency events the process is a little different. Here's how it typically works:

1. The call usually comes to Scott or Dick and a quick decision is made without holding a board meeting.

2. An emergency email is sent out to the Team. The coordination of the events depends on the special circumstances involved with the emergency effort.

3. The LCT has supplies palletized for certain types of emergency events. Among the items are cases of water, paper goods, disposable goods, utensils etc. These pallets of supplies are ready to go at all times.

Sometimes the hardest thing to manage for these events is food. The LCT has grown to have a large forty-five foot long containerized walk-in refrigerator/freezer. We keep a limited amount of frozen items inside. These items can be cooked or re-heated in these cases. It's a unique feature other organizations don't have.

Recurring Holiday events such as New Year, Easter, 4th of July, Labor Day, Thanksgiving and Christmas present opportunities to raise money. They allow you to pre sell food such as briskets, ribs and turkey in bulk.

Chapter 10

Communication with Your Team, Sponsors and the Community

As with any successful organization, communication is critical to ensure everyone's on the same page and the word gets out to your community about what you're doing. There are many great ways to communicate. Below are communication tools that have served the LCT well.

Email Newsletter to Keep People Informed

- Send out an electronic newsletter every quarter. *Low Cost Tip: Build your contact list by collecting business cards at events and fundraisers*. LCT sends out a quarterly news- letter. Online tools like "Constant Contact or "Mail Chimp" make organizing and sending out your newsletter easier.

- Printed newsletter: The LCT prints a few copies of their newsletter to use as a handout for educating new spon- sors and volunteers. The format for the LCT's newsletter is an eight and a half by eleven inch size with a cover, two inside pages and a back page. Its printed in color by a sponsor who pays for it.

    o The front page of your newsletter will feature your in- formation: name, logo, address, phone number, etc.
    o The inside content will include past and future events and other newsworthy items about your organization.
    o The back page lists your sponsors.

Videos Help People Feel the Good You Do

A picture is worth a thousand words. Spread the word about your organization through a video. It's a great way to attract new vol- unteers and attract sponsors to what you're doing as well. Make it inspirational and heartwarming. Make it humorous and real. Don't scrimp on your video. It can be a great way to recognize and celebrate volunteer efforts. Videos can be costly to produce, but we've discovered the cost is offset through donations from people who were inspired to help out once they saw our story.

To see our video go to www.lighthousecharityteam.com. Below are tips for creating your video:

Include photos of your events. Everyone takes "selfies" these days which can be a great source of pictures of volunteers working hard, having fun and the charities you help with big smiles, maybe wiping away a tear.

- Interview your volunteers and sponsors in your video and have them tell their own stories in their own words of why they got involved with your organization and what they get out of it.

- LCT has made two videos which provide a great way for us to share our People Helping People message and mission. The cost for each ranged from five to eight thousand dollars but has been worth the investment.

Your Charity's Social Media Presence

Having a social media presence is critical to good communication in today's world. No matter the medium, Facebook, Instagram, or Twitter, it's a great way to communicate with your volunteers, sponsors and community. Make sure to include this type of communication in your plan.

Getting Positive Media Exposure

- Local Newspaper- call the local newspaper and invite them to your event

- Local and Public Access Television – contact producers for a show that features local event. Especially if your event ties into a larger news story in some way.

- Radio – write up a PSA (public service announcement) or ask the show producer about being a featured guest on a show.

- Community Bulletin Boards – post a flyer about your event on them. Bulletin boards can be found at municipal buildings, grocery stores, coffee shops, etc.

- Thank your sponsors by taking out a congratulatory ad after the event

It may sound like a lot of work, however, if you take it one step at a time you'll get there and you'll be surprised how quickly everything comes together. Positive energy and enthusiasm at the beginning and as you grow will make a big difference in accomplishing the tasks outlined in Chapters 8, 9 and 10.
Ask yourself, "What will keep me motivated along the way?"
Think about and remind yourself of your reasons "Why?"

Why are you doing this? Think about the happy smiles, the sense of community your events will build and the people who'll benefit because you made a firm decision to put your passion to work and bring upbeat, heart-centered, service-minded people who want to help along with you. Take a deep breath and accept the fact that this work will change the lives of so many.

After all, who doesn't love good food? Whether you're "cooking for a cause" charity specialty includes barbeque, fried chicken, delectable pastries or – perish the thought – clean, healthy food, people will be drawn to what you're doing. Everyone has to eat, right? What's better than eating and helping someone less fortunate at the same time? The people served will benefit in so many ways.

Nicolas Maynard - Cancer Patient

When Nicholas was four years old his Grandmother called to ask for our help. Her grandson Nicholas was diagnosed with cancer. His mother was forced to quit her job to take care of him. He was a patient at the University of Texas Medical Center in Galveston, and would be undergoing numerous outpatient treatments.

Just starting out in life this young family lived in a mobile home in Dickinson, Texas. Even with their modest lifestyle they couldn't afford to live on one salary. Responding to this heartfelt request, the LCT came to their aid. We hoped with our funds, they could keep afloat despite the loss of the second income and crushing medical expenses.

The LCT held several more events for Nicolas and his family. The first event was held at the V.F.W. Hall in Dickinson and raised over fifteen thousand dollars. Several months later another joint fundraiser with the Dickinson Methodist Church and other kind-hearted community residents netted over 25,000 dollars.

We were then asked to cook for the Hughes Road Elementary School at the end of the school year. We served hot dogs and soft drinks.

About a week later, Scott received a stack of "Thank You" cards from Nicolas' elementary school. The Principal, Mary Hollis, asked the students to each send a card to our Team for helping their classmate and friend. Below is Nicolas' card.

We lost contact with the Maynard Family for a few years. One day the LCT was cooking at a Crawfish Boil in Dickinson, when a young man came up to me and said,

"Hi Mr. Daugird, my name is Nicolas Maynard and I want to thank you for helping my family years ago." He was with his family and girlfriend. This strapping young quarterback of the high school football team was cancer free. It reminded me, yet again, why we do what we do.

Chapter 11

Fundraising Begins at Home

You've outgrown your facilities and need to expand. Now you need to raise funds to sustain growth.

With growth business strategies must be adapted. From a small organization feeding fifty people at local events, the LCT grew to eventually have the capability of feeding five thousand people in one event. With growth, came the need for more resources, especially money. It became more than sponsors could provide. So, a decision was made to host their own fundraising event so the Team could continue its work. This was a new concept - the LCT raising funds for themselves. Over twenty years they increased their funding from fifteen to over 400,000 dollars per year. They did it by hosting their own fundraiser. Below are LCT's guidelines for hosting your own fundraiser. Ask:

- A local restaurant or food wholesaler to supply the food for your event
- Volunteers from organizations you've helped to attend your event and help out. This will allow your own volunteers time to meet, greet, and visit with guests
- Local radio and television personalities to be Master of Ceremonies. They'll do a great job telling your story to everyone present.

Below are a few fundraising ideas that have worked well to raise necessary cash and gain a little extra exposure for the Lighthouse Charity Team over the years:

Banquets with local bands, national recording artists or professional athletes. Include a silent and live auction and sell raffle tickets to give away free items.

Become a charity of choice for civic organizations such as Rotary and Lion Clubs. These organizations look to help their communities. Become that need.

Host a golf tournament to promote your organization. This type of event will be more effective as your name is established and you garner enough sponsors to purchase teams. Through the teams, which are typically friends or clients of the sponsors, you'll give more people a chance to see and understand what you do.

They may in turn become volunteers and/or sponsors. We want our sponsors to have fun, so we include competitions such as:

The longest drive
- Closest to the pin
- Putting contest
- Hole in One

Ask local merchants to donate items for the golfers' "goodie bags." We provide lunch, a gourmet dinner and a concert following the tournament.

- LCT has partnered with boating events such as sailing regattas and poker runs.

Matching fund programs have helped. When an employee donates money, their employer matches employees' donations. Hour per hour donation: When a company employee performs community service, some employers will donate an agreed amount for each hour worked to the charity.

Scott shares a recent fundraising success

A recent example of a golf tournament fundraiser that worked well utilized a unique angle. We not only raised funds for the LCT, but also honored one of our long-time supporters. We've mentioned our relationship with the Del Papa family in Galveston several times throughout these pages. We wanted to host a golf tournament for Lawrence Del Papa, an icon in the Galveston community. Over the years his wise counsel and generous nature helped many people during his lifetime.

We approached Larry, Lawrence's son and president of the Del Papa Distributing Company and asked if we could honor his late father. He was touched by our request and suggested the tournament be held on his father's upcoming birthday.

On a hot July day, we brought the Galveston community together to remember this great man. Our event was a resounding success. Once again the LCT volunteers, sponsors and donors showed their loyalty through their participation. That evening we hosted a concert and dinner to complete the event. This allowed many others, who don't golf, to attend and honor one of their heroes.

This is an example of when you do good for others, they will be there for you. Through this gesture, we honored a man who left a true legacy in the community while raising funds to continue our own work.

The event generated almost 40,000 dollars which was applied toward our operating budget. Attendees, along with our sponsors and donors, know that money will go a long way toward helping the LCT's ongoing expenses for maintenance, insurance, utilities and the four salaries we pay to run our operation.

Our community understands and values our contribution. We've worked hard to earn their faith and trust because we operate at a bare-bones cost and give maximum dollars back to our community.

Chapter 12

A Tribute to Our Military and First Responders

In August of 2016 we were asked to help with the "Back the Blue" campaign to support the families of the slain police officers after the shooting in Dallas that took five officers' lives. It was to be held in Galveston with hundreds expected to attend.

The horrible rampage unfolded in real-time in downtown Dallas on news channels nationwide and internationally. It left a huge gap in the Dallas police department as well as for the friends and families of the officers slain that day. We had to jump in and help despite short notice and a full calendar.

Overcoming the numerous logistical and unexpected issues that arose, we successfully served more than one thousand people that day who showed up to pay tribute to these slain officers and their families. At the end of the day we were the honored recipients of a US Flag flown over the United States Capitol on September 11, 2015, along with a Certificate Signed by our Local US Congressman commending our contribution.

Earlier we dedicated a chapter to stories and testimonials from veterans and first responders who help LCT and are a vital part of our team. In this chapter we'll share a bit about ways like the example above where we've helped local police officers, veterans and first responders with fund-raising events to show community support. Dick hails from a military upbringing and recounts how his respect for the military became a part of who he is as a person.

My father served in the US Air Force over 25 years before retiring with honors. As a child, we lived on various U.S. Airbases including bases in Japan and England. The Lighthouse Charity Team has always sought opportunities to be involved in events that supports our men and women in uniform. The gift of safety and freedom these heroes provide should never be taken for granted.

We look for ways to stay connected and support our military brothers and sisters. In that spirit, Horacene and I decided to purchase eight Military Field Kitchen (MKT) trailers.

The Daugird's personally purchased three Deuce and a Half Military Trucks and eight Military Field Kitchen (MKT) trailers for the use of the Team.

These are real working kitchens and once the mainstay of overseas food service for our troops. This equipment can be found in military salvage yards. When rebuilt, they're capable of feeding three hundred people per meal and small enough to be towed behind most pickup trucks. We retrofitted these military trailers to hold a rotisserie pit, "KP" dishwashing trailer, a fifteen-kilowatt diesel generator, sleeping trailer and more

MKT's make great starter cooking trailers. They operate off of a generator using diesel, kerosene or jet fuel. Or, simply plug into a 110 AC outlet. They have a griddle and range for boiling water or cooking and baking. You can keep on cooking through almost anything since they're equipped with bad weather walls, mosquito netting, handrails, and a rain canopy. Horacene and I bought these trailers from govliquidation.com and ebay.com. The price ranged from eighteen hundred to over six thousand dollars each depending on their condition. We also purchased three, "deuce and a half" trucks to pull the MKT's. The cost for each truck was sixteen thousand dollars.

In addition to using this equipment for cooking, we also set it up as a static display during parades, and special holidays. We watch proudly as families who attend these events ask questions and take pictures while adults tell stories of their own military family members serving or who once served our country. Whether it's Veteran's Day, Independence Day or Memorial Day, this equipment stands as a reminder of the men and women who fight for our freedom and safety.

For years we've been involved with the 147th Air Wing at Ellington Field. I remember our first event, "Welcome Home Troops, Operation BBQ." It was such an honor to be on the flight line as these soldiers came home to see their families who they hadn't seen in months. We served four thousand troops, spouses, kids and anyone there to welcome them home. That first event led to many more, allowing us to show our appreciation to these great men and women.

The military never forgets. During our massive cooking effort for Hurricane Ike, Scott received a call from the Colonel at Ellington Field. He asked, "Could y'all use a little help with the work you are doing there in Galveston?"

Scott responded, "Yes, sir, we sure can!"

The following day several white government vans pulled up to our facility. Dozens of men and women in matching uniforms walked in asking, "Who's Scott?"

Everyone pointed towards the kitchen, curious as to why all these uniformed personnel were looking for Scott.

Approaching Scott, they announced, "We're here to thank you for everything you've done for our brothers and sisters in uniform. What can we do to help?"

Our weary volunteers couldn't believe it. After feeding thousands of people since the hurricane, they were exhausted. The troops immediately jumped in and tackled the dirtiest tasks. They washed dishes, equipment and floors, while our tired volunteers took a break. With their help, we prepared and served over 3,500 meals in eight hours that day.

Our relationship with the 147th Air Wing at Ellington Field is one of ongoing friendship and respect. The troops donate their time as waiters and waitresses at our Annual Fundraiser. They consider helping us an honor and they do it with pride. As with all military personnel, they do it to perfection.

Other events for Military and Emergency Responders

We've participated in several Veterans Day celebrations at Galveston's Submarine Park, home of the retired WWII destroyer Stewart and submarine Cavalla. We typically serve chili for up to 400 active and retired veterans and guests.

After Hurricane Ike roared through Galveston Island inflicting damage on thousands. National Guard troops were summoned to help the LCT. We served over 30,000 meals at First United Moody Methodist Church to residents whose homes flooded. Free lunch and dinners were served daily, for a month with drive-through pick up service.

New York Life, among other companies, sent employees to Galveston to help with serving.

Veteran's Day at The Veteran's Center in Galveston. The gentleman on the right, Gene Nevelow wearing his USAF hat, is a 34-year veteran of the USAF. He declared he was 95 plus 185 days old. I guess if I reach that age I'll count my age in years and days, too.

The gentleman carrying the flag is our Team Member, Larry Spurgeon.

"Bikes for Vets" is a program designed to help those who don't or can't drive. We provide those military men and women free bicycles to help them be more mobile and get around the island.

Houston Police Department's Air Support Division

In 1980, Houston Police Officer and one of my insurance clients, Gary Daniels, called to say he was accepted as a helicopter pilot for the Houston Police Department's Air Support Division. The helicopter division patrols a 700 square mile area of Houston. They have two helicopters in the air or on duty for up to 21 hours a day manned with Houston Police Officer Pilots and Tactical Flight Officers.

Gary offered Dick a two-hour patrol ride in a helicopter and Dick accepted. After the ride Dick asked Gary, "Is there an opportunity where the LCT can cook for your squadron?"

Gary forwarded the request to his superior. Since the captain was unfamiliar with Dick and what the LCT did, he wondered why an insurance man would want to help the Police Department. He proceeded to get Dick's driver's license information to investigate his authenticity. The investigation went well, and the LCT has been cooking an annual free Christmas Dinner for this elite group of men and women for 26 years now.

Tank Explosion in Galveston, February 12, 2012

A crude oil tank exploded and was burning at a biodiesel plant on the waterfront docks in Galveston. Firefighters responded quickly to keep the neighboring tanks cool and prevent more explosions. It was a dangerous situation and fellow firefighters from nearby Texas City and La Marque rushed in to help their Galveston counterparts.

The LCT was called in on short notice and stayed until the fire was out. In the first picture Horacene is feeding Firefighters dinner at 1:00 a.m. in the morning.

The Rig

Horacene and Dick originally purchased this motorhome. Later, it was donated to the Team for an offsite operation center and command post. Todd Nelms with JMH Blast Coat donated the custom paint job and Scott retrofitted the interior to suit the needs of the Team.

Team Members Dave and Sue Gillioz purchased a new motorhome for LCT events. They had the Lighthouse Charity Team name applied to all four sides. The RV is used as an additional command center. It serves well as a place to change clothing and secure personal items during events. Thanks, Dave and Sue.

Watchfire - Dave and Sue Gillioz liaison for Lighthouse Charity Team

The Watchfire tradition originated from the military. Following a battle or long march, a large fire would be lit so those missing or lost troops could locate and rejoin their comrades. Once a year, using that time honored, symbolic model, the LCT uses the warmth and light of our own Watchfire to guide everyone to join us. We reflect on our fallen comrades without whose service and ultimate sacrifice America wouldn't be as strong.

Vietnam Veterans use the Watchfire and accompanying cere-mony to make Memorial Day more meaningful for people in the community. We invite Veterans and Non-Veterans to gather at the Watchfire to honor those who so faithfully served the nation and given their all for our freedom and independence.

The Watchfire also provides the community with an opportunity to respectfully retire unserviceable American flags. People who join in are encouraged to bring tattered, worn or faded flags for respectful burning on the pyre. LCT provides food and drink.

USS Texas Submarine Commissioned

The USS Texas arrived at Galveston Bay September 4, 2006 and was escorted into the harbor by Galveston's resident tall sailing ship Elissa. With a crowd of 10,000 people in attendance, the USS Texas was commissioned in Galveston and joined the U.S. Atlantic Fleet on September 9, 2006.

It was quite an honor for our Team to cook for the crew and VIP'S attending this commissioning. We spent an hour just getting our Team Members and trailers through the security protocols. Many of us met the commander and crew and witnessed history in the making.

Lone Survivor Foundation Event at Crystal Beach on Bolivar Peninsula

This foundation restores, empowers and renews hope for wounded service members and their families. The Lone Survivor Foundation, with the help of Brint Construction and the Bolivar community, opened their first retreat at beautiful Crystal Beach.

Retreats are conducted by an experienced team of behavioral consultants and specialists incorporating education, stress reduction activities and relaxation and accommodate 28 retreat functions a year, helping up to 225 soldiers and veterans.

This worthwhile endeavor provides a healthy environment for soldiers and veterans to learn from others experiences and develop methods to move beyond the negative impact of active engagement.

The LCT is going on our fourth year cooking at Frogfest on Boli-var Peninsula, a major fundraiser for the Lone Survivor Facility. Country crooner Jerry Jeff Walker performed at the last event and proved he loves Bud Light.

http://lsfcrystalbeach.kintera.org

Comments from our First Responders

Bob Wieners, Chief of Police for the City of Friendswood 2001

My introduction to Lighthouse Charities and Scott started in 1997. I was on active duty in the Marine Corps back then. The unit I was assigned to came into Friendswood to help search for Laura Smithers, a 12 year old girl who was kidnapped. We were here for several days, and as a Marine I enjoyed the meals they prepared during our tough assignment.

When I got off active duty, I came to work for the city of Friendswood in the police department. Over time, we interacted with the
LCT on multiple community events. One event I especially remember was Tropical Storm Allison in June of 2001. We lost 144
homes during that storm and they helped out with storm relief
operations. They were there for the initial flood and stayed
through the post-flood recovery. They served their community
again during Hurricanes Rita and Ike. Seems they show up every
time the Galveston country or even surrounding areas had a
natural disaster. Lighthouse has always been there and supported the first responders:

- The Police Department
- Our firefighters
- And our EMS crews.

They're an all-purpose volunteer organization that saturates itself
in the community at both micro and macro levels, depending upon what's happening. No job is too small or too big. They're willing to step into whatever needs to be done.

They have a lot of depth in their core volunteer group. Everyone's a hard worker. As they've grown, they've stuck to their
core mission of *People Helping People* and stayed on track.
They've never lost sight of their original cause because they continue attracting the best people.

Josh Rogers, Captain of the Criminal Investiga-
tion Division, Friendswood, TX Police Department.

I connected with Lighthouse Charity Team in 1999 through various community events they participated in ranging from the Fourth of July parade to large-scale disasters. Their team of cookers, servers and clean-up folks would show up at the scene to feed first responders like firefighters and police officers I was one of those.

We showed up today at their volunteer appreciation event as a police department to thank them. Recently, they've assisted us at two separate dig sites where we were recovering human remains in Harris and Brazoria counties. Their help was invaluable. They showed up and immediately built an air-conditioned command center with food, water, and bathrooms.

We were at the Houston dig site for 25 straight days, literally working around the clock. They made this tough assignment more bearable. Not only did they man the command center the entire time, their volunteers also took the time to visit with the officers taking a break to eat. This took our minds off our gruesome task if only for a little while. It was a huge relief not worry about food, water and shelter.

When the LCT shows up, they're not looking for anything. They come to help and they deliver. This organization is so successful, due to their can-do attitude of service and the satisfaction they get from helping others. The folks who gravitate to Lighthouse seem to have this in common. Like any private business or charitable organization, you are who you recruit. Employees and volunteer become your best ambassadors. They've grown because of the culture of the organization and the work they do in our community, always with a mindset of serving and helping. It allows them to have a much bigger footprint than when they first started out.

Robert J. Horton, CM Sgt, TXANG, Superintendent, TMO, LGRD, 147th Reconnaissance Wind, Ellington Field

I've been a friend and volunteer with the Lighthouse Charity Team for over ten years.

I first met the Team at a Family Day event held at Ellington Field Air Base twelve years ago. As we were planning it, we looked for someone who could cook and assist in the day's activities. After meeting Scott and the Team, we knew we found the right people. It was obvious, from our first meeting they care about community and service members alike. I was sold after hearing all the good things they were doing to give back.

Since that first event at Ellington, we've done a number of events together. The bottom line is they care. It's been a great partnership and they've done a lot for our soldiers. That's why I enjoy giving back what I can.

One way we give back is by joining them at their Annual Fundraising Banquet. I ask for volunteers from among my group. Together we work alongside the LCT serving meals to over 600 guests, supporting the Lighthouse Silent and Live Auctions. As a Team Member of LCT, it's nice being included on all communications about upcoming meetings and events. Some I can attend, others I can't, but it's good being included.

Like the military, any great organization must have good leaders. Dick Daugird and Scott Gordon are exemplary leaders. Scott always greets me when I arrive at meetings and both he and Dick have the Team's respect. Without them, the LCT would not be what it is. I believe you can sum up who the Lighthouse Charity Team is in three simple words: *People Helping People.*

Chapter 13

Final Thoughts from the Founder

Dick comments, "The LCT was founded on our love of cooking and feeding others. We now cook for a cause. Actually we cook for many causes. We live and breathe our mission of *People Helping People*. Many young children we helped raise money for years ago are now grown up young men and women contributing to our community. The number of people who've joined Horacene and me in this endeavor humbles me. These people are friends and family. Many folks aren't included in this book, due to size limitations. Your omission doesn't devalue your contribution in any way. You, and we know who you are and your contribution counts… both in this life and in the ever after.

As a youth, I never could've predicted my passion for cooking would serve our community so well. As a volunteer stated earlier, it's the dream of most people to make their mark in this world. I'm proud of not just the contribution Horacene and I have made, but I have even more pride when I think about the thousands of people who've joined our cause and contributed to its success along the way. We simply couldn't have done it without you. Going forward you'll be the continuing reason for our success.

Looking into the future I have no crystal ball. Who knows what's next? The ultimate vision for LCT is to feed people who need a helping hand and a good, hot meal on the moon. With our belief system as strong as ever, and with Scott leading our team, LCT will continue delivering what we call POS, Positively Outstanding Service."

Lorraine states, "I'm grateful for the opportunity Dick gave me to share the powerful story of the Lighthouse Charity Team. Through Dick, Horacene and countless volunteers' tireless, selfless efforts, this small town charity has grown to become a significant contributor to the welfare of people throughout the state of Texas. My intention co-authoring the book was to validate what I already knew about the impact of Putting People First. Volunteers are unpaid, but they put in more hours doing their "job" because they genuinely *want to* help and not because they *have to* help. The LCT's winning formula could be replicated within any organization or community. You just have to care."

Resource Guide

The resource guide contains four areas:

1. Facts about Lighthouse Charity Team
2. Current cooking Equipment List
3. Event Option Ideas to Get Started
4. Health Codes for Food Operation

Facts about LCT

1. Principals
   a) Dick Daugird, President
   b) Horacene Daugird, Secretary/Treasury
   c) Scott Gordon, Vice President

2. Unlike many non-profits, the officers are volunteers and don't receive a salary. Each officer spends at least sixty hours a week on events, planning, administration, maintaining and replacing equipment and other tasks.

3. The LCT never charges a fee for the use of its equipment, nor do they charge for the volunteer labor provided for fundraising events.

4. We primarily help non-profit organizations, schools, churches, people with medical needs, and emergency response efforts due to weather or manmade disasters, to name a few. We handle approximately 80 events annually.

5. We do not cater, nor do we compete in cook-offs.

6. LCT's first event in 1984 was a Labor Day Telethon for the Muscular Dystrophy Association.

7. Over 100 volunteers stand ready to help out at a moment's notice.

8. Our annual budget is approximately 500,000 dollars.

9. Funds to cover our expenses are obtained primarily from individual and corporate donors.

10. We hold one major Fundraiser each year. Our last Fundraiser was at The Knights of Columbus Hall in Pearland, Texas with a 600 people who paid 200 dollars each in attendance. The dinner is donated by Gordon Food Service and served by The Ellington AFB National Guard with beverages donated by Del Papa Distributing Co. A live auction with many donated items is held. Past entertainers have included national recording artists like Tracy Lawrence, Mark Chesnutt, Kevin Fowler, Tracy Byrd, Doug Stone, and Darryl Worley.

11. The LCT has branched out into providing meals in Emergency Response situations. We're the first ones called by local Police and Fire Departments for "food on site" for their men and women. We're fortunate to have the support of our local Police, Fire and EMS as Team Members and friends.

12. We can provide food and beverages for emergency responders on short notice. We'll have a trailer with hot food from our commissary on site usually within one hour of an emergency.

13. Our slogan is *People Helping People*

14. The McRee Ford dealership has donated seven new commercial trucks for pulling our trailers over the past 20 years.

15. AMS Houston has donated and also maintained all our air conditioning and refrigeration needs.

16. Adobe Equipment has donated two forklifts, one for Friendswood and one for Galveston to unload palletized food trucks for our walk-in cooler.

17. Over one million hours have been donated by our volunteers to helping local non-profit organizations.

18. The furthest distance traveled to an event was in Nashville, Tennessee in 2010 and 2011. Our Team prepared Thanksgiving Dinner for eight hundred men, women and children staying at a shelter after being displaced from their homes. Twenty dedicated volunteers gave up their own holiday dinner with their families to help this worthwhile cause.

19. We have many repeat requests due to the success of our events.

20. To volunteer, go to www.lighthousecharityteam.com

21. Contact information: Scott Gordon 281-482-9400.

22. Our office is located in a Lighthouse in Friendswood, TX.

23. Volunteers and Sponsors have remained loyal to us for many years, despite the ups and downs of their personal businesses.

24. Larry Del Papa, the Budweiser® Distributor in our area donated the use of a   22,000 square foot, air conditioned building, complete with furnished offices.

25. Volunteers build and maintain our trailers.

26. We overcame a major fire that wiped out our Friendswood building, equipment, trailers and inventory, incurring about one million dollars in damages.

27. Many loyal Team Members forego birthdays, anniversaries, family events and more to help other people in a time of need. This demonstrates dedication and a commitment to our *People Helping People* mission.

28. Over the years we've received awards such as:

- Community Leadership Excellence
- Volunteer of the Year
- Unsung Hero
- Multiple City Proclamations
- Citizen of the Year
- Charity of the Year
- Key to the City
- Grand Marshall at the 4th of July Hometown Parade
- Texas State Resolution from the House of Representatives

Mobile Cooking Equipment – Current Inventory

- 30, custom trailers
- 2, self-contained 45-foot motorhomes used as a command center and to house personnel on site.
- 1, Bunkhouse Trailer currently under construction. This is a converted MKT with raised and closed in walls, insulated, air conditioned, with two sets of custom made

bunk beds and a bathroom. It will provide additional sleeping quarters for four Team Members.
- 6, Ford F350 and F450 Trucks (Late Model-one ton or larger) for towing trailers.
- 1, Refrigerated Truck w/ a Lift Gate
- 1, Ford Service Truck with Tool bed, Welder, Air Compressor and a 5000 pound Lifting Crane
- 7, MKT'S (Military Kitchen Trailers, each designed to feed 900 meals daily).
- 3, High water military Deuce and a Half rescue vehicles
- 2, Refrigerated Trailers
- 3, Forklifts for unloading palletized food and paper goods.
- 1, Motorized riding floor scrubber
- 3, Golf carts for moving volunteers and supplies on site.
- 6, Pallets of bottled water on hand
- 1, Pallet of 1-Gallon jugs of bottled water
- 1, 45-foot Container Refrigerator/Freezer in building for holding food.
- 4, Generators: 25KW, 40KW, 60KW, 60KW
- 300 Gallons of Propane on site
- 300 Gallons of Diesel on site.
- 1, Water Trailer - a converted generator trailer with a 275-gallon food grade IBC (Intermediate Bulk Container) for carrying water for cooking and drinking, most often used in a disaster location.
- 1, Trailer with a Culligan 1,500-gallon per day Reverse Osmosis System for water purification.
- 1, 20-foot Tandem axle trailer for moving palletized water containers to site.
- 1, Forklift dumpsters for trash

Event Options to get started

To get an idea of the kinds of events possible, here is a list of past community members and events the LCT has participated with and in. These are only a few of the thousands we've participated in.

Emergency First Responder Support (Firefighters, Police, etc.)

- Injured Firemen
- Injured Police Officers
- Fundraisers for Fire / Police Equipment not in their budget
- Family Day for Local Military Departments
- Coast Guard Recognition Ceremonies

Community Fundraisers

- Boys & Girls Club
- Little League Sports Teams
- Booster Clubs at Local Schools
- PTO Clubs of Local Schools
- Spring / Festivals
- City Sponsored Day in the Park
- Sea Scouts
- Boy & Girl Scouts
- 7 on 7 Basketball & Football Organizations

Church Fundraisers

- Support of Church Festivals
- Local Church Oktoberfest
- Senior Citizen Organizations

Civic Organizations

- Lions Club
- Knights of Columbus
- Kiwanis
- Rotary Clubs of America
- Masons
- Feeding of the Homeless/Working Poor
- Special Needs

Medical Patients

- Children with Long Term Diagnosis and in need of financial help
- Children with Sports Injuries

- Families with medical patient in the household needing care

Emergency Response - Feeding first responders is as important as feeding emergency victims

Natural Disasters – Hurricane, Flood, Earthquake, Blizzards, Wild Fires, Train Derailment, Road & Bridge Collapse.

Man Made Disasters –Explosions, Chemical Plant Issues, Structure Fires where long term presence is needed by emergency staff.

Health Codes

Even as a charity, you'll be held to the same health code standards of any restaurant. Check with your local health department for your specific permitting requirements. Here are a few (but certainly not all) the things they typically check:
Cooking equipment (temperature controlled heating)

- Refrigeration units
- Sinks (must be sanitary)
- Fresh water supply
- Holding tanks
- Food Storage
- Ice Machines
- Serving line

LCT prides itself on delighting health code inspectors. We put a great deal of effort into ensuring the quality of our food. Over the past 32-plus years no event has ever been shut down due to improper food handling. *Low Cost Tip: To learn about what inspectors look for, call your local health department and ask if they offer food-handling courses. Then send your volunteers. The cost is usually reasonable since the charity may not have the extra funds, volunteers will pay for it themselves.*

As we draw to a conclusion, since we're a cooking team, it wouldn't be right to close out this book without sharing a few of our favorite recipes. Despite thousands of different meals cooked, we have a few tried and true "favorites" we love. Our cornbread recipe hails from one of our volunteers' grandmother who started baking it way back in 1930. Each of the recipes are guaranteed to be a hit with any crowd you're serving. We share them with you in the hope that you'll enjoy them and share them with your community. For these and more recipes, visit our web-site, www.lighthousecharityteam.com.

Contact Information

We have written this book to explain the history, the direction and the guidelines followed by the LCT to become the charitable organization we are today. We hope to help others build a similar "Charity Cooking" concept.

We're here to offer assistance whether you're an individual, a group, a civic organization or non-profit, or you just want to im-prove your community.

Lighthouse Charity Team Members will happily provide an initial consultation to you at no cost. Our professional services include community development, kitchen and equipment design, recipe and event planning, etc. If you require us to make a personal visit to your location for a meeting, we only ask you to cover our travel expenses. Our mission is helping you get started and as-sist you in making your goals of helping others a success in your area.

Our expertise in designing and building portable cooking trailers for others was unexpectedly put to the test when Gordon Bethu-ne, CEO of Continental Airlines contacted us in 2000. He heard about our custom portable cooking trailers and wanted LCT to help him design and fabricate a barbecue pit on a trailer as a replica of a Boeing 777 airliner.

I accepted the challenge and, relying on the expertise of the LCT, submitted the design to a manufacturer in Missouri. Hora-cene and I flew to Missouri every two weeks to supervise the construction. Six months later, the barbecue trailer was com-plete. We had it transported to Houston where it was quickly entered in the Houston Livestock Show and Rodeo and the Pas-adena Rodeo where it promptly took first place honors.

We were proud when it was featured on an episode of the Dis-covery Channel. It toured the country for the next few years and was a showstopper everywhere it went. To the best of my knowledge it is still roaming the country winning awards.

For more information regarding any of our resources such as forms, contracts, printed matter and guidance on starting your own cooking charity, please contact us.

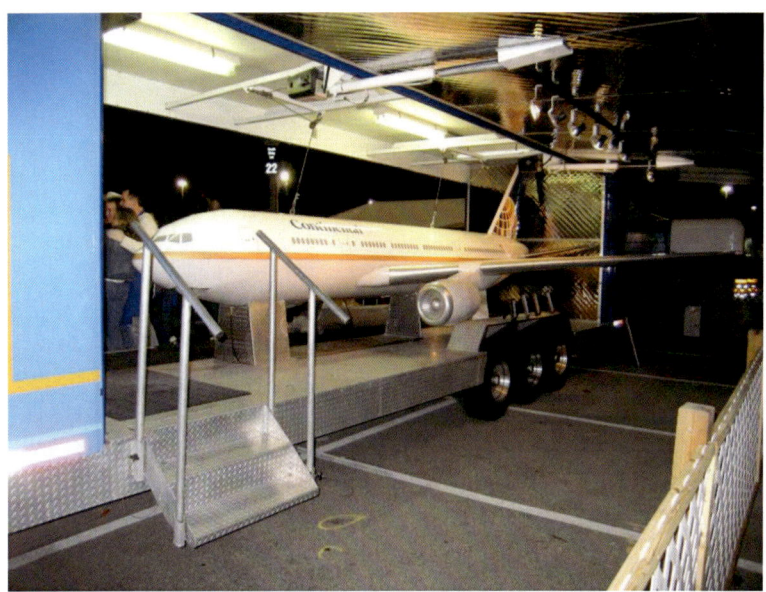

Contact Information

Lighthouse Charity Team
Friendswood, Texas
www.lighthousecharityteam.com

Scott Gordon, VP
lgthse@swbell.net

Dick Daugird, President
dick@daugirds.com

Lorraine Grubbs, Co-Author
lorraine@lorrainegrubbs.com
www.lorrainegrubbs.com

TO OBTAIN A COPY OF OUR BOOK:
Go to: www.lighthousecharityteam.com,
www.lorrainegrubbs.com or amazon.com

"People Helping People"
The Lighthouse Charity Team

In Memoriam

Alton (Captain Wick) Elsworth Rouse, 1934 - 2013

An eighteen year resident of Dickinson, Texas and long-time resident of Seabrook and Kemah, Captain Wick was a mechanic and worked in the marine industry all of his life. He could fix anything and loved helping people.

Captain Wick founded the tradition of the Blessing of the Kemah Fleet. He was a very generous person and donated his 72 foot boat to the Lighthouse Charity Team. He is survived by his wife Alison Rouse.

Dick and Scott, who each hold a 100 Ton Captain's License, have donated many trips to other non-profits for their fundraisers.

The 72' Captain Wick boat was donated to the Team in 2002.

Stephen "Steve" T. Brown, 1947 - 2013

Steven was born in Tyler Texas and is survived by his loving wife, Dolores Brown. Steve had many passions throughout the course of his life, including sod farming, NASCAR racing, traveling, sailing and piloting their airplanes.

He served his country by joining the United States Army during the Vietnam War.

Steve and Delores donated their 33' sailboat "Zena" to the Team. In addition, they always attended our annual Fundraisers and helped by donating week long, all-expense paid trips on their 42' Leopard Sailboat "Sugie" berthed in the Abacos, Bahamas.

The Brown Family continues as a great sponsor of the Lighthouse Charity Team.